Judy Barron
and
Sean Barron

THERE'S A BOY IN HERE

FUTURE HORIZONS INC.

ARLINGTON, TEXAS

There's a Boy in Here

Emerging from the Bonds of Autism

All marketing and publishing rights guaranteed to and reserved by

FUTURE HORIZONS™ INC.

721 W. Abram Street
Arlington- Texas 76013
800-489-0727
817-277-0727
817-277-2270 (fax)
E-mail: info@FHautism.com
www.FHautism.com

Printed in the United States of America.

ISBN 10: 1-885477-86-4

ISBN 13: 978-1-885477-86-6

ACKNOWLEDGMENT

I would like to thank my father for his years of understanding and for spending thousands of hours of his life talking to me. Finally, I heard him. I would also like to thank my sister, Megan, who helped me more than she will ever know.

—Sean Barron, 2002

For Ron and Megan Barron
For the memory of Mildred Johnston Welch

FOREWORD

Since our book was first published in 1992, my life has changed in ways I couldn't have anticipated. In the past ten years I've traveled the United States and Europe, speaking to many civic, church and social organizations about what it was like to have autism and to recover from it. Along the way I've become friends with many children with autism and their parents. Before the book came out I had never met anyone else with the disorder.

Shortly after the book's first release, Doug Biklin invited me to speak at Syracuse University. It was the first time I had ever given a presentation at a college. I was nervous, sensing that people would be scrutinizing my actions and words to see whether I was fully recovered as had I claimed. When I began to speak, though, I immediately felt comfortable and confident; the audience was more responsive and accepting than I could have imagined and I felt as if I were talking to a large group of friends.

That was the day I first saw facilitative communication being used. I was stricken by the way it allowed non-verbal children to express their thoughts and feelings. A 24-year old woman who could make only sounds, not words, particularly moved me. With her facilitator's fingertips resting on her shoulder, she wrote me a message conveying what she couldn't say: she apologized for the involuntary noises she had made during my speech and gave me a series of poems she had written. Her writing, from a woman whose thoughts could not be spoken, was beautifully expressive.

My own writing has changed in ways that mirror my recovery. The more I recovered, the more the "abstract" side of my brain opened, allowing me to see the world from a wider point of view. I no longer perceived other people's words literally, nor their actions in black and white. I was not satisfied with simple answers to complex questions and issues, and I began to see the subtleties in relationships and connections between people and events outside myself. These were refreshing changes for a person who had hated change of any kind.

A few years ago, after giving a talk in Mississippi, I was introduced to a 14-year-old boy with Asperger's Syndrome. His mother told me that her son wanted to be like me when he grew older. I was stricken by how much he looked like me when I was a teenager. Although he kept his back to me as we talked, he asked pointed and intelligent questions—something I had never done at age 14. He was interested in learning about my job and my hometown, and he wanted to know how it felt to talk in front of so many people at one time. After I'd answered his questions and he stood up to leave, he suddenly turned and looked directly at me. We shook hands. I felt a shock of warmth as I realized I had made a real connection with him.

Our book has been translated into nine languages, most recently Icelandic. My mother and I went to Iceland to give presentations in two different cities. While there, we visited a school with a class of seven teen-agers with autism. The staff was remarkable, treating each child with dignity and respect, like especially gifted students. In general, the people of Iceland seemed to accept autistic behavior as "normal," and I left wishing I had had that kind of acceptance during my childhood.

I've made many friends among those who have phoned or written to me about their children. After meeting and speaking with so many parents, it's clear that they are dedicated to doing anything they can to help their kids. Many have said their son or daughter does the same things I did when I was small. I do my best to explain what was going on with me, hoping it will help them better understand their own children.

Recently I have taken my writing further by working as a copy editor and a reporter for our local newspaper. I have written many features in addition to more traditional news stories and I enjoy the work tremendously. I have re-enrolled at Youngstown State University where I'm working towards a 4-year journalism degree.

In recent years I have grown even closer to my family; they are three of my best friends. The second-greatest gift I have ever received was the publication of our book.

Recovering from autism was the first.

Sean Barron
Poland, Ohio
November 2001

PREFACE

In 1965 my husband and I were told that our four-year-old son, Sean, was autistic. We had never heard the word before. We were also told that his behavior, which was uncontrollable, would get worse—that by the time he reached puberty he would have to be institutionalized, that we would wish he had been born blind or deaf or retarded, because those were all things for which parents could get help. With autism, nothing could be done. Autism was hopeless.

That was twenty-six years ago. Like most people who receive that kind of news, we refused to accept it. We read everything we could find about kids like Sean, though little was available. We went to professionals for help and used the tranquilizers they prescribed, followed the programs they devised, used the behavior modification methods they insisted on. None of it made any difference. We were treated with condescension, we were patronized, we were even threatened with a future of doom. Through it all we kept asking questions, of ourselves and of them.

No matter what the statistics said, despite the horror of the prognosis, we caught rare and fleeting glimpses of a helpless child trapped inside the bizarre behavior of Sean's autism, and we were determined to get him out. Eventually we turned away from the professionals and followed our own instincts and common sense. We used everything we had—our love, our rage, our

Preface

frustration, patience, inventiveness, violence, ignorance, and humor. The process of "reaching" Sean was messy, terrifying, filled with regrets and guilt. Most of the time we didn't know what we were doing, just that we had to keep doing *something*; we were sure that if we gave up and let go, our son would be lost to us forever.

Somehow it worked.

For seven years Sean has been living by himself in his own apartment. He has graduated from college, has a full-time job in the rehabilitation department of a retirement home, drives his own car, has a girlfriend, plays tennis, and spends his free time working as a volunteer with several service organizations and listening to his collection of vintage jazz records.

Several years ago Sean said he would like to be able to help other families that are going through the same hell that we lived in for so long. At the age of twenty-five he decided he wanted to write a book about what it's like to be autistic. He has, as a result, brought to the surface the pain of his childhood memories—the terror, confusion, and isolation—to try and explain what autism is really like from the inside. I have kept a journal for years, a written account of a life we lived but never understood. That journal is the basis for this record of our chaotic, tumultuous life as parents of an autistic child. Together Sean and I have written the story of his release from the terrifying imprisonment of his own mind.

—Judy Barron

I eased slowly out of the hospital bed and stood up, shivering when my bare feet hit the cold linoleum. Carefully, I crossed to the black-specked mirror and looked at my grinning face. "You're a *mother!*" I said aloud. Was such a thing possible? "You've got a son, Sean, a baby boy," I told my reflection. I was overcome with a radiant joy that a moment later was cut with a stroke of fear. *Me,* a mother?

Ron came into the room and stood behind me, wrapping his arms around me. We both looked into the mirror. "Our baby has a twenty-one-year-old mother and a father who looks twelve instead of twenty-two!" I laughed. He kissed the back of my neck. "Do you feel strong enough to walk down to the nursery and look at Sean Chapman Barron?" he asked. Of course.

We stood in front of the glass window and stared at our baby. He was bigger than any of the others and looked older— perhaps because his birth had been three weeks late. A flood of mixed feelings washed over me: I had given birth and lived through it! (I had been sure I would die on the delivery table.) We had a healthy and robust baby! But how could I be responsible for anyone so small as this when I didn't even feel like an adult? And I knew absolutely nothing about babies, had never even held one under six months of age! Who was this strange being about whom we knew nothing?

They brought him into my room for feedings in a metal cart

on wheels. "Don't go to sleep now and roll over on him," one of the nurses said. "It's easy to crush a baby that way." He quickly drank the liquid from the little bottles and still seemed hungry. Was it enough? They obviously know what they're doing, I thought.

Sometimes he wouldn't wake up and a nurse would bustle in and say, "Thump his feet to wake him—like this! Don't worry, it doesn't hurt them!" Why didn't it?

When a nurse took him away, the hours were long and surreal. I tried to read, but my mind wandered; I couldn't focus. I lay and listened to the cries from the nursery—one continuous, persistent wail cut through the other sounds. Whose baby was it and why didn't they quiet it? The sound was frightened, forsaken. I would never let *my* baby cry like that.

Ron and my parents came to the hospital to take us home. I was up and dressed, sitting in the obligatory wheelchair like someone who had been seriously ill, though Ron and I had been walking the halls for a week. A nurse brought our baby in and handed him to me.

"Here's the noisy little fellow," she said. "He never did shut up in the nursery—guess he thought he wasn't getting enough to eat! We did give him extra bottles, though—he sure has got some appetite!"

"You mean he was the one crying all the time?"

She nodded, laughing.

"But why didn't anyone tell me?"

"Oh, there was nothing you could have done."

That night Ron and I stood with our arms around each other at the foot of the crib. I looked around the room, Sean's room. Until tonight it had just been "the baby's" room. I had painted every room in our new house; it took months, and by the time I was through, my eight-months-pregnant stomach was so huge that I couldn't reach the baseboards without lying on my side. I had saved this room for last. Ron had built shelves for toys and books, and he'd made the blue-and-white print curtains for the windows. It was perfect.

We watched our baby as he slept. He was so tiny, a perfectly formed human being with the potential to be or do anything in the world. How funny to think that he didn't even know us yet, nor we him. And yet we would share our lives, the three of us.

I smiled at my feelings of anxiety. How hard could it be, I thought, to take care of a child. Untold millions of people had done it before us in every imaginable circumstance, many with less intelligence and fewer advantages than we had. We would love him, respect him, teach him with kindness and patience.

"Isn't it funny," Ron said softly, "that a person that small can change both our lives?"

I got out Sean's new set of wooden blocks, the perfect toy for my fourteen-month-old toddler. Since he had learned to walk, though, he had hardly toddled—he moved so fast he was usually a blur. I dumped the blocks onto the living room floor and sat down beside them. "Let's build a tower, Sean!" I said to him as he whizzed past, not seeming to notice the new toy. On the next pass I stopped him and plopped him down next to me. I busily began stacking blocks on top of one another, but Sean had another idea. He grabbed several blocks and put them on a tabletop. Then he knocked them off onto the floor, throwing himself down to watch them fall. Immediately, he repeated the process. Odd, but harmless, I thought. He'll soon tire of that. He did it again, and again, and again. And again. Each time he put the blocks on the table and swept them off, he became more enraptured.

"Honey, come here and play with me," I said gently, taking his arm. He shook off my hand, piled more blocks on the table, and knocked them off. This time he got the lamp cord, too, and I caught it just before it fell.

"No, Sean. No more. Come sit here with Mommy."

He twisted away and took another block, replacing it on the tabletop. I took him by the shoulders and moved him away, putting the block back on the pile on the floor. He whined, not looking at me, and reached for another handful.

Running to the table, he plunked them down and knocked them off.

"*No, Sean,*" I said again. I took his hand firmly and sat him down on the floor with me. I'm wise to this, I thought—it's just a battle of wills; he's trying to assert his new independence. "Look, help Mommy build a tower." As soon as I let go of him he leaped to his feet with a block and put it on the table, immediately whisking it into the air. "*No, No!*" I said loudly. I took both his hands and drew him away. Holding him securely I tried to make him look into my eyes. "No, Sean. Mommy says *no.*" He twisted his head from side to side, never meeting my gaze. It's just something he has to learn, I told myself, but of course there's no contest: I'm bigger, stronger, older, and more clever. With patience and firmness I will teach him that there are some things a child can do and others he cannot. Simple as that.

By the time Ron came home from teaching school that afternoon, the lamp was shattered, the table scarred, the blocks in the closet, and Sean in his room. With what voice I had left, I tried to explain. I had given up on the blocks, gathered them and put them in the closet. As I was doing that, Sean picked up a stuffed animal, put it on the table, and swept it off. I took it away. I held him, face to face, and tried to make him look at me; he wouldn't. He was giggling strangely under his breath, an eerie sound. I said to myself, *I am a twenty-two-year-old woman and I will not lose my temper with a fourteen-month-old child!*

I took him into his bedroom and got out some crayons and paper. "Let's color!" I said cheerily. He shoved my hand away and ran from the room. When I reached the living room in hot pursuit, he was setting up two crayons on the table for their flight. I scooped him up. "*No,* Sean. We're going outside for a nice walk."

I bundled him into his snowsuit as he fought to get away from me. I carried him outside into the cold Ohio winter air and set him down on the sidewalk. It was almost time for his nap, and the weather wasn't good enough to stay out very long, but I knew that a change of scene and the fresh air would distract him.

I chatted with him as we walked, pointing out the wind-driven clouds, the neighbor's dog, the color of passing cars. We reached the corner and turned back toward home. When I opened the front door he rushed past me, grabbed a toy car, and set it on the table. *Whooosh!* It flew through the air.

"You're silly—you have a one-track mind!" I said as I took off his snowsuit in spite of his struggles. "It's nap time!" I announced as I carried him to his room. When I began to remove his shoes, he whipped several crayons off his play table with his arm. He threw himself to the floor to watch them fall, giving me a painful kick as he did. I plopped him into his crib and sat beside him to read a story, something to calm us both. I showed him all the pictures, but as always he didn't really look at them.

I kissed him and left the room. He slept; I stewed. I had been, I realized, really furious with him, and that was clearly ridiculous. He was only a baby and I could certainly be more patient with him than this—teach him the meaning of "no" without getting so angry. After all, he didn't know what he was doing and could hardly be blamed. If I got angry, how could I expect him to trust me?

When he awoke I picked him up and held him tightly, filled with remorse. I gave him a snack in the kitchen, then lifted him out of his high chair and set him down. He trotted into the living room, picked up a small wooden animal, set it on the table, and knocked it off.

"No, Sean. We'll play with your circus animals the right way." The rest of the afternoon we were locked in combat.

I said no, no, no, *nooooo!* I moved him away from the table, hundreds of times, trying anything I could think of to distract him. Nothing worked. My noes got louder and louder. He knocked over the lamp again; I caught it. Except when I restrained him physically, it was as though he were alone in the room—he didn't look at me, didn't seem to hear me, didn't hesitate to put anything he could onto that damned table! When I stood planted in front of it, he used the one across the room. When I had taken away every toy he could pick up, he used kitchen spoons.

What was I doing wrong? I sat slumped on the couch, my teeth clamped together, my heart racing. I watched him. Without my interference he was so happy, so completely absorbed in what he wanted to do, giggling oddly to himself. He seemed unaware of my presence; he never glanced at me.

I rejoined the battle. Springing to my feet and wresting the spoon from him, I yelled *"no!"* He didn't react. While I was putting away the spoons he ran into his room and found a handful of crayons. I came back into the living room just as he swept them off the table, this time getting the lamp as well. I lunged for it but it was too late—it fell to the floor and shattered.

I grabbed Sean and spanked him, several times. His eyes barely flickered over mine. I carried him to his room, dumped him into his crib, and glared at him. He was unfazed.

Closing the door behind me I went back to the living room to clean up the glass. At first I didn't realize I was crying, but tears of frustration and rage and humiliation ran down my face. I knelt on the floor, defeated. I had struck my own child, a baby—something I had sworn never to do. Bubbling under all the other feelings was terror—nothing I had done to stop him had made even the slightest difference.

Could this be the way kids act at this age—a "phase" of some sort? If so, how did other parents ever put up with it? It's me, a cold voice inside my head suddenly said. I just don't know how to handle a child. What is wrong with me?

But it wasn't a phase, I knew that. I thought back over the past year and had to acknowledge that there were too many other signs. I had always been baffled by Sean's reaction to being held—he squirmed and twisted uncomfortably, pushing hard against me as if he felt trapped. He never snuggled up to my body and held on as it seemed all the other babies I saw did. He always cried a lot and nothing I did satisfied him—not changing his diaper, not feeding him, certainly not picking him up and holding him.

When he was only two months old Ron and I had set up his playpen, round with soft corded sides, so that we could put him in that instead of on the rug while we tried to eat dinner. Mealtimes were a nightmare—nothing would stop his incessant crying. Once in the playpen he would lie on his back and "climb" the mesh sides with his toes, pulling himself into the air. Then he'd let go and thud onto the floor, crying desperately. We tried holding him on our laps at the table, but he flailed about, crying. We both worked at getting dinner ready, taking turns trying to quiet Sean, but nothing helped. When we sat down to eat—our first time all day to talk, my first chance for adult conversation—we couldn't hear each other, couldn't think, couldn't swallow.

Finally, after an evening of failed attempts to distract or quiet the baby, he would exhaust himself and fall heavily asleep. In the sudden silence I would feel battle-weary; my body tingly and my ears ringing.

It wasn't hunger—when Sean was two weeks old the pediatrician had told us to feed him not only baby cereal but baby fruits and vegetables as well, and Sean ate huge quantities of everything. The doctor had even prescribed a medication that would relax the valve in Sean's stomach that made him "think" he wanted more food than he really did. When I said that the crying and the enormous amount of food he ate worried me, the pediatrician looked at me benevolently and pointed out that my baby was growing, gaining normally, and had rosy cheeks.

Why did he cry so much? I asked. Didn't babies cry for a reason? Because they were hungry, wet, or sick? It wasn't colic, the doctor assured me, and indeed Sean didn't sound the way babies do when they're unwell; his cry sounded, I thought, terrified. But how could that be? What could he be afraid of . . . me?

During Sean's first year the days were the longest I had ever known. I was lonely and isolated, always exhausted. Adding to my isolation was the fact that I didn't know anyone else with a baby. I had lost touch with my high school friends, most of whom had moved away, and our neighbors were older couples with grown children. I spent all my time with the baby, doing everything I could think of to comfort him, entertain him, love him. Sean was a large child and he grew rapidly. I loved watching him learn to do new things—to turn over, to sit up— but he barely responded to me. Instead he stared fixedly at toys that spun, at moving shadows, at blowing curtains. Though the incessant crying had stopped when Sean was about four months old, he still cried a lot, and still for no reason we could think of. When he wasn't crying I could not get his attention. He almost never looked at me.

When I set him down on the floor he picked at the fibers of the carpet with his fingers. He was fascinated, never taking his eyes off his hands. He seemed hypnotized. I'd call to him, try to get him to look up, to reach out for my hand, for a toy. At most his glance would flicker over me and he'd return his attention to the rug. I had asked the doctor about his hearing, but it was clear that was not the problem. I could see for myself that his ability to hear was acute but selective—he might not respond to his name, but if the furnace came on or the refrigerator made a noise, no matter how faint, he heard it instantly and stared in its direction.

I talked to him constantly. I told him everything I knew and then some. I babbled, hoping he'd listen, look at me, laugh. And he did laugh sometimes, but I never knew at what. By the end of the day I knew I was invisible.

A seed of an idea planted itself in my mind then sprouted and grew into a conviction: He doesn't like me. With the uncanny knowingness of babyhood he senses that I'm not a good mother, that I don't know what the hell I'm doing, that I'm a total failure.

Every night when Ron came home I would be flooded with relief. He took the responsibility for the baby out of my hands. Often he cooked dinner when I had no energy to do it. (This isn't fair, I thought. He's out working all day, and when he gets home he has to do the work here too; I, on the other hand, have been home all day with nothing to show for my time.)

With Ron there, the feelings of frustration and failure I had felt all day almost evaporated. I was being silly, I told myself—

no doubt this was the way all new mothers felt; I was simply insecure and inexperienced. Ron was sympathetic and reassuring, and the evenings were restorative.

"I'm sure it's just a phase of some kind," he said more than once. I'd nod. But I could see a fear in his eyes that didn't match the comforting words, and I'd look away.

After our baby was asleep Ron and I talked every night for hours. We talked about everything—his experiences at the school where he taught English, the books I was reading, family incidents. But for a long time there was a subject we didn't talk about—we were both afraid there was something wrong with our child, and we couldn't bring ourselves to say those words.

Since we were still living in Poland, Ohio, the small town where we had both grown up, we often saw our relatives. Large family dinners, with aunts, uncles, cousins, were excruciating. Sean cried from the moment we arrived; he would not be settled or soothed. We said he was fussy, that he was tired, that he was afraid of so many people at once. Everyone was tolerant—they spoke softly, tried not to overwhelm him, smiled, tried to help. When nothing worked they all pretended it was perfectly normal to eat dinner with a screaming baby and his two parents, whose faces were beaded with sweat. Embarrassment filled the room: ours at his behavior, our inability to know what he wanted and comply; theirs, we thought, because we could not control our own child.

We'd leave as soon after dinner as we could, Ron and I with pounding headaches and severe indigestion. Usually Sean would become quiet and fall asleep as soon as we got to the car. On the way home we would vow never, never to do it again, never to put ourselves and our baby through that. But a month or so would pass . . . he was older now, they would say; it was a holiday and we couldn't keep him away from his own family; this time it would be different, they knew. It was always the same.

Physically, Sean was progressing at a better-than-average rate. I checked my Dr. Spock book. It warned me never to compare one infant with another because each grows and develops differently, but it gave me the charts to compare with. Our baby was bigger and heavier than others his age. By six months he was up on his hands and knees, ready to crawl. When he wanted to move, though, he flopped back down on the floor and pulled himself along with his forearms, like an infantryman. He was drawn to odd things. He'd crawl past a brightly colored selection of toys to get to the furnace register. Once there he would stick his fingers into the slots and watch his fingers move. There was a hole in the wooden floor of his bedroom that riveted his attention. He'd put his finger into that and wiggle it around for hours. What the hell was he doing?

Just after his first birthday Sean had learned to walk. About fifteen minutes later he learned to run. Ron and I thought it was the most amazing thing we had ever seen—our baby had turned into a little boy! I found that I was running a lot, too, trying to keep up with him. His new mobility brought about a lot of changes.

One night we noticed a peculiar smell in the house—it was strong and it was everywhere at once, as if a cathedral's worth of candles had all been extinguished at the same time. I happened to notice that most of Sean's crayons were missing from the can where I kept them. I frowned, looking around the room. Suddenly I knew where they were. I knelt and examined the furnace register in the living room—sure enough, there were traces of melted crayon on the edges of the grille. Ron looked at me. "He's thrown his crayons down into the furnace, hasn't he?" The answer was only too obvious. We turned and looked at Sean. "No, no!" I said. Ron picked him up and looked into his eyes. Sean looked away. "Sean, you cannot do that again," he said firmly. We were to live with the smell of melted wax for the next two years.

Fixing dinner one afternoon, I heard the toilet flush, followed by Sean's strange giggle. I ran to check. He was standing in a pool of water on the bathroom floor, the toilet overflowing all around him. I sloshed past and pulled up the plunger to stop the water. Since we had only one toilet, I called our plumber, who arrived within the hour. He had to break the seal and remove the toilet, but he found the problem—a brand-new bar of soap, still in its wrapper, was lodged in the trap. His visit cost $40, an amount that was staggering to Ron and me. However, we were to pay that $40 repeatedly over the years because of a variety of objects—blocks, tinker toys, a baby shoe, a washcloth—that Sean flushed down the toilet.

One of Sean's favorite activities was turning light switches on and off. He would turn the switch until we stopped him, but we could not stop him for long. He'd just find one in another room. One morning he stood at the bottom of the attic stairway flipping the light on and off. I said no but he didn't notice. Oh, what the hell, I suddenly thought; why fight him? After all, he's not really hurting anything—it's better than some of the other things he chooses to do. So I pretended not to notice, curious to see how long he would keep it up. Maybe, I thought, if I don't pay any attention, don't correct him, he'll lose interest—maybe he just does these things as a kind of perverse way of getting my attention, negative though it is.

I busied myself in the kitchen, ignoring the strobe-light effect coming through the doorway. I could hear his giggle. I made it through fifteen minutes before I ran to the stairway. He didn't see me; he was staring at the flashing light as if he were in a trance. He looked like someone I didn't know, like a robot. I scooped him up in my arms, filled with guilt, and carried him into the bedroom to read him a story. He fought me all the way.

I remember lying on the floor picking at the carpet with my fingers. It's one of the first things I do remember. The feel of something that was not perfectly smooth was wrong to me—I picked at anything that did not have a solid surface. One rug in our house had many small ridges; by scratching them I could tell that all of the rug was the same, even if it looked different. I had to keep picking at it to be sure that the whole rug was the same, all of it. It must not change!

When I was a little older, I felt terrible walking around the house in my bare feet. It felt strange and awful to stand up and be still when I had no shoes on. My feet were extremely sensitive. So, when I had to be barefoot, I tucked my toes underneath so I could pick at the carpet with them. No matter how many times I touched the rugs, I kept on doing it to reinforce my feeling of security and to reassure myself that the rugs were the same each time.

I loved throwing crayons down the registers. I was fascinated by the holes in the registers as well as by the darkness of the holes themselves. It was impossible for me to see where the openings led and how far down they went. I'd throw a crayon into the hole and then listen for the sound it made when it hit bottom. Sometimes I just loved looking through the register, so I'd stick my finger through the metal covering and reach in as far as I could. It made me mad that I couldn't lift the cover off and use my whole arm. The more I wondered where the passage went, the more mysterious it got. I absolutely had to know where the hole went, how big the tunnel was, and what the end of it looked like, but I was afraid I would never find out.

I was pregnant. Our second child was to be born in November. It was another easy pregnancy, but I was tired all the time. Keeping up with Sean, watching him every second as he sped through the days, was impossible. He needed constant supervision, and there were no quiet times when he was involved in some harmless activity. If he was awake, he was moving.

Though he was a year-and-a-half old, I couldn't get him to play with anything or to sit while I read to him. In the afternoons I'd sink into a chair in the living room and put my feet up. As soon as I did, Sean began to run like a caged animal, from one side of the room to the other, as fast as he could go. He did it forty-five, fifty, sixty times, and my head would begin to ache as I watched. Why was he so frantic? My mother said: Boys are like this; they have too much energy for their own good sometimes; he just doesn't want to be "cooped up" in the house.

My mother loved her first grandchild unreservedly, and her presence had a most positive effect on him. Didn't his behavior seem odd to her? I explained that he wouldn't do anything I told him to, that I couldn't stop what he did no matter what I tried. She said I was overreacting, that she could get him to behave when he was at her house—maybe, she suggested, Ron and I were asking too much of him for his age.

Then it *is* me, I thought. There's something wrong with *me*.

"Besides," she continued, "if he doesn't behave when he's

with me, I just tell him, 'Sean, if you do that again, I'll have to send you home!' " (That very afternoon I tried it. After he had bounced toys down the stairs, flicked toothpicks down the register, turned the lights on and off a thousand times, and emptied a new bottle of shampoo down the bathtub drain, I said to him, "Sean if you do that again, you'll have to go home!" He actually looked at me for a moment, puzzled, then dashed away. I knew I was probably losing my mind, but how I enjoyed that moment!)

I decided I had lost my perspective. I simply had to stop focusing on the negative. True, everything Sean did was repetitious, most of it destructive, but still there were a lot of things he did not do. After all, we knew parents of a child Sean's age who had needed to thread chains through all the handles of their kitchen cupboards to keep their son from getting into them. Other kids barely out of infancy spent all their time watching television, but our son never did. Some children hit their mothers! It could be so much worse, I told myself. Sean was beautiful and highly coordinated. Perhaps he was simply bored—though he had lots of toys, maybe they just didn't interest him. One day, when our son had become a dedicated scientist, Ron and I would laugh to think how much we'd worried when all along our child actually had been investigating the principals of gravity, experiencing the limits of physical laws.

No one else saw anything wrong. I talked to the pediatrician about Sean's behavior; I said Ron and I were powerless because he paid no attention to us. "Oh, you'll learn," he said, smiling reassuringly. "It's always hard at first." I forged on. "But what about the food he eats? He won't touch any fresh fruits or vegetables and he won't eat them cooked. All he wants are starches—cereal, bread, mashed potatoes, macaroni, spa-ghetti—and all of it in huge quantities. Should I allow him to eat ten or twelve pancakes at a time? He can't be that hungry, it must be a craving of some kind."

"I had a patient," he said, "a four-year-old. His mother was going crazy because he refused to eat anything except Chef Boyardee spaghetti from a can. I told her, 'So feed it to him! When he's had enough he'll eat something else.'" He patted me on the shoulder and walked me out of the office.

I got the message. Relax, he was telling me, you're making this harder than it really is. It was the same message I got from my mother: Don't make everything such a big deal. My mother had reared two children, the doctor had worked with thou-sands. They had to know what they were talking about.

But only Ron and I lived with Sean day in and day out. Our son was nearly two years old and he paid no attention to anything we said to him. I'd yell; he'd ignore me. He wasn't defiant, he just didn't seem to notice me. To get his attention at all I had to grab him and shake him, and over time the shakings had gotten harder and harder. I had violated my promise to myself never to strike my child so many times that I'd lost count, and the smacks had turned into real spankings. If I hit him hard enough he would sometimes look at me. I had to get through to him somehow, I thought, and if that's what it took, then I had to do it.

He showed not a single sign of remorse. When I spanked him he got furious, as if I were in the wrong, as if I were some maddening obstacle he had to contend with. He had to know by now, I thought, what we didn't allow him to do, yet he continued to misbehave right in front of me, without sneaking, without hesitation. Hating the physical violence, we put away

18

things he misused, telling him what we were doing and why. When all his toys were gone he didn't notice—after all, there were always light switches, and we couldn't do much about those.

Ron and I believed ourselves to be reasonable, gentle people. We seldom argued, never raged at each other, and couldn't stay angry for more than minutes. We searched for a way to discipline Sean constructively—we wanted to teach, not to hurt. We came up with a way. When he refused to listen to us, we decided, we would simply make him sit on a chair in the living room for a few minutes until he realized he had to do what he was told. There would be no more yelling in our house.

After dinner that evening Sean took the big wooden pieces from one of his puzzles, piled them on a chair, and knocked them off. I took away the puzzle. He began pulling books off a shelf and dropping them on the floor. "No, Sean," Ron said. No reaction. Ron picked him up and set him on the designated chair. "*No, you can not do* that. Now you sit here until I tell you to get down." Sean got down.

Ron returned him to the chair. "You *sit* here." Sean got down again. Ron grabbed him and put him in the chair again, hard. He held Sean there while he struggled frantically to escape. Finally he was still and Ron let go. Sean got down. Ron put him back with a thud. Sean screamed—he was outraged, furious.

"Don't!" I cried, "He's not old enough to understand. He doesn't know what we want of him!" I wanted it all to end.

"Oh yes he does—he just won't give in and do what he's told," Ron said. He held our son on the chair, talking steadily to him, explaining the same thing over and over. "If you do something bad and don't stop when we tell you to, you will have to sit on the chair." After several minutes, Ron released him.

Sean slid down from the chair without a glance at either one of us. Within minutes he was bouncing toys down the attic stairs.

But Ron and I weren't fools; we knew that parents had to be consistent with kids and, God knows, patient. We spent that evening and many that followed setting Sean on the chair. The result was always the same. We didn't impress him, it was abundantly clear. Surely, we thought, he would eventually get the point—if he refused to listen to us he would have to sit on the chair. But each time he was as furious as ever, jumping down as soon as we let go, as if we had no right to correct him. As if he just didn't get it. Our nonviolent method had turned violent.

Our certainty that with time we would get through to him eroded and was replaced by the realization that what we were doing was senseless. He reacted exactly the same way the fiftieth time we punished him as he had the first. Was he, for whatever reasons, just too young to grasp what was happening? Or did we have a child with something missing—a conscience, a capacity to understand consequences? We gave up on the chair.

I loved repetition. Every time I turned on a light I knew what would happen. When I flipped the switch, the light went on. It gave me a wonderful feeling of security because it was exactly the same each time. Sometimes there were two switches on one plate, and I liked those even better; I really liked wondering which light would go on from which switch. Even when I knew, it was thrilling to do it over and over. It was always the same.

People bothered me. I didn't know what they were for or what they would do to me. They were not always the same and I had no security with them at all. Even a person who was always nice to me might be different sometimes. Things didn't fit together to me with people. Even when I saw them a lot, they were still in pieces, and I couldn't connect them to anything.

I remember my mother telling me not to do things I loved, like, "Don't throw crayons down the register!" I have a very good memory, I think. But what she said had no meaning because what I wanted to do blocked out her words. I didn't understand the consequences of my actions, nor did I care about the consequences one bit.

My attention was on what I was doing at the time: 100 percent of my focus was on that. I vaguely knew my mother was around, but I wasn't really aware of her unless she did something bad to me—like yelling or stopping me from doing what I wanted. She was not important.

Thinking back, I believe that when I was a child, up to the age of five or six, I would not have been able to pick out my mother from a group of other women. I never really looked at her. She was more or less a presence I felt rather than saw, a negative presence. So was my dad, really.

They made me sit on a chair sometimes. It made me so very angry! I recall that they said words to me, but that's all they were, just words. I don't think I even knew what they meant, but it didn't matter. They were interrupting me and interfering with me, and I wasn't doing anything wrong.

"You've got a baby girl this time, Mrs. Barron!" I looked at the unbelievably tiny being that the doctor placed on my stomach. I had been sure we were having a second son and was overwhelmed at the sudden realization of how very much I had wanted a daughter. My eyes filled with tears.

Megan looked impossibly frail, birdlike. She was born a month before Sean's second birthday, and I was worried and apprehensive. What would he think of her? How would he react? What if she were just like him? Throughout my second pregnancy I had been tormented with nightmares and, even worse somehow, with sudden images that would flash through my mind in the middle of the day—images of a mutilated baby, of Sean attacking me with a knife. Though Sean was never hurtful physically to anyone but himself, how could I know what he would do? I knew nothing whatsoever about him.

Sean came to the hospital with Ron and my parents to drive us home. He appeared to have doubled in size in the five days since I had seen him. In the car on the way home he stared fixedly at me, for the first time in his life. We held the baby up for him to see, but his gaze never wavered. I smiled at him, reached out to touch him, but he shrank away, still staring. I tried to read his expression—it was as if he were watching a stranger doing something incomprehensible.

But my immediate fears for Megan's safety seemed un-founded. Sean simply didn't pay any attention to her; I don't think he noticed that there was a new baby in the house. She was easy to care for, easily satisfied by being changed, fed, held. So this, I caught myself thinking, is what it's like to have a baby! Most of my time was still spent watching Sean, who continued to do whatever he liked. I ran after him saying "no" over and over, yelling "no," grabbing him, shaking him. Two or three times, however, I did succeed in getting him to look at his new baby sister, and once he actually reached out and touched her. I was thrilled.

Now that we had a new baby, we were deluged with relatives. They dropped in whenever they were out shopping, on the way home from church, or just driving by. With visitors around, Sean's behavior became markedly worse—as if he sensed that I was restrained by the presence of someone else—and as soon as the doorbell rang he took off for whatever activity was currently making me the angriest. He'd grab a piece of silverware from the kitchen and gleefully set about sliding it down the register right in front of us; he'd get the broom and stand it up until it was balanced, then let it fall—he liked it best if it whacked him on the head as it fell, and no matter how hard it hit him, he never failed to giggle.

The relatives responded as if he were being silly, "rambunc-tious." But after a few unsuccessful tries at "Sean, come over here and sit beside me!" their faces would stiffen, they'd look away, and, as much as possible, would ignore him for the rest of the visit.

One afternoon while Megan took her nap, I decided to bake a banana cake, Ron's favorite dessert. It was tricky—the last few I had made looked wonderful as they came out of the oven but a few minutes later had caved in and turned to goo. This one, though, was perfect, in spite of the fact that I was interrupted every few seconds by having to chase Sean down and "correct" him. I had spent all afternoon fighting with him, screaming at him. I was filled with resentment that I couldn't do anything without his constant interference, and I was disgusted with myself, with my lack of control, of patience.

The doorbell rang. I peeked through the curtain and saw my Aunt Hazel on the step. Since I knew she had to have heard me yelling, I could hardly pretend we were out, and besides, with our only car at school with Ron and the icy Ohio winter outside, where could we be? I welcomed her warmly.

As soon as she sat down in the living room, Sean flew past us into the kitchen and turned on both taps in the sink full blast. The rushing water hit a large metal spoon and became a fountain. When I ran to turn off the faucets, there was water running down the wallpaper and cupboards, dripping from the ceiling, and lying in a pool on my freshly baked banana cake. Something snapped. I cornered Sean and spanked him as hard as I could, shaking with fury. He was silent.

Taking some deep breaths, I went back into the living room and rejoined my aunt. She smiled as though she had noticed nothing—my family's way of dealing with unpleasant situations in general. We said a few things to each other while I wondered why she had come—she was not the sort of woman who had time to stop in and visit.

"Well," she said finally, "aren't you going to show me the new baby? I haven't seen her, you know."

Baby? Oh my God, the baby! I'd forgotten there was one! I went to get Megan from her crib, where she was awake and gurgling happily. When I picked her up I was crying. What kind of mother could forget she had a new baby?

When my mother came home with the new baby I was rather confused. What was she doing here? I didn't think that the baby would be staying with us—that didn't enter my mind. I couldn't understand why nobody came and got her. I know now that my mother had talked about the new baby before it was born, but I didn't know what her words meant at the time, and I didn't connect what she said to this new baby. I never knew she was my sister until a long, long time later.

When we had visitors in our house I felt that the threat of being interrupted would be removed for a time. I felt safer when there were other people in the house. I didn't care about them or even look at them, but I knew my mother would have other things to attend to. I would get to do what I wanted for a longer period of time.

We tried to outsmart Sean, to outguess him, removing things that he could misuse from the house. I tried to think like him, to imagine what kinds of objects and activities appealed to him and divert them into some sort of "healthy" game. It was an exercise in futility and only made me realize what a stranger our son was.

The most innocuous items became the focus of our struggles with him. There was a wall phone in the kitchen beside the table. The first time he noticed it, the result was spectacular. I had fed him, then prepared Meg's bottle and my lunch so that I could feed her while I ate. I went to get her from her crib, and when I returned a minute later I found her bottle lying on the floor and my lunch everywhere else, most of the soup splattered on the curtains. Sean had, as I saw a moment later when he repeated the action, pulled the telephone cord out as far as it would reach, then let it go, clearing everything off the table. We wrapped the cord tightly around the phone's body; he unwrapped it. I wrapped it again and taped it so it wouldn't dangle temptingly; he unwrapped it. Should we take out the phone?

In the bathroom he loved to hit the roll of toilet paper, making it spin until all the paper was curled in a massive heap on the floor. Should we stop using toilet paper?

I decided to try to talk to my mother again. She was the one person in the world Sean did respond to—he allowed her to touch him, even hug him occasionally. He was visibly more relaxed at her house; though his behavior was the same she could sometimes divert him, grabbing his hand and taking him outside with her, away from the pieces of elbow macaroni he'd taken from her cupboard to flip down the register. She pretended not to notice; was that what I should do?

I described his blind persistence in the face of everything we tried to do to stop him. "But all kids do things like that," my mother said, "especially boys. He's still too little to understand, and I think maybe you're being too strict with him." But, I protested, all kids may do these things, yet not all the time, not these things and nothing else! She didn't want to listen anymore; I was making her uncomfortable. I'd begun to feel as if I were building up a case of some kind against my own child, an excuse for myself because I couldn't control him. It became clear that although I thought there was something wrong with Sean, my mother thought there was something wrong with me.

Though he was more than two, Sean still wasn't talking, nor did he babble the way other kids seemed to. One day, however, we overheard him muttering to himself what sounded like a series of numbers, though we couldn't be sure. A few days later Ron and I stopped to get some bread at the corner bakery with Sean. While waiting our turn we heard a little voice: "Eleven-sixteen-thirty." Ron and I looked down. Sean was staring up at the large clock that hung over the counter. Ron said, "He has just told us the time to the second." Indeed he had. We were thrilled—words at last, and he could tell time already! When we later asked him what time it was, though, he didn't answer. He didn't seem to know what we meant.

He would sit at the kitchen table with a knife and fork, moving them into various positions like the hands on a clock. "Four twenty. Two ten." Sometimes he set up the "hands" at a particular time, said (for instance) "six-fifteen," and then moved himself around the table so that he saw the knife and fork from the opposite direction, at which point he'd say, "nine-thirty." We were amazed. But why wouldn't he say anything else?

As Megan grew through her first year she was a delight to be with. Water was her favorite element, and she dove and swam underwater in the bathtub when she was only a few months old. Each night we both emerged from her bathtime equally wet and happy. She laughed easily and often, responding to everything around her. She adored books and would sit on my lap endlessly while I turned the pages and read or talked to her. I couldn't get over it—how wonderful actually to be able to play with and cuddle one's child!

She was fascinated by her older brother, reaching out for him whenever he came near; he paid no attention to her but she didn't seem to mind. She laughed at his activities and became instantly sobered when I had to reprimand him. I hated to see her smile disappear at the harsh sound of my voice.

I suffered from an increasing resentment that my time with Megan was always cut short or eliminated altogether by Sean's behavior. As soon as I sat down with her I tried to have him sit with us, to listen to a story, look at the pictures. But he'd be off and running—to the light switches, the sink, the phone cord. Again and again I thought: What the hell, I'll let him do what he wants. Who cares if he destroys everything we own? I'd see him becoming frantic, obsessed, like a wind-up toy run wild, and I'd have to go to him, shake him, stop him. I yelled until I was hoarse.

In August the four of us drove to Lake Erie to spend a weekend with my parents at a cottage they rented. Next door was a little boy, Jay, who, at two-and-a-half, was exactly Sean's age. I couldn't take my eyes off Jay—he was active, alert, responsive, friendly, and highly verbal. The difference between him and Sean was astounding. This will be great for Sean, I thought—it's just what he needs; he'll see the way Jay talks, asks for things, does what he's told.

It was our first holiday since the kids were born, and we spent the first day on the beach. Eight-month-old Megan was crazy about the water. Although she had never been in anything larger than a bathtub before, when Ron carried her into the lake she pushed away from him and swam fearlessly into the waves, dogpaddling like mad toward Canada. When we thought she'd had enough sun and tried to take her out of the water, she screamed with such fury that we covered her with a big T-shirt, stuck a hat on her head, and let her swim.

Jay spent the whole day following our son. At first he tried to interest Sean in playing with toy cars and digging in the sand, but he got no response. Sean picked up handsful of sand and let the grains run through his fingers, then went back to the things he always did. Jay joined in. By the time the sun set on Lake Erie that evening, Jay had stopped talking and was grunting instead. The next day his mother kept him at home.

By her first birthday Megan was walking and saying a lot of words. She quickly moved on to sentences. We hoped Sean would begin to say something, to imitate her, but he stayed with grunts and numbers. Since he was large for a three-year-old, people tended to speak to him as if he were even older, then were visibly surprised when he not only didn't answer but went into one of his incomprehensible activities. Countless times I was told, "Well, you know Einstein didn't talk at all until he was four, and of course he was a genius!" (To this day I don't know if that was true, but everyone in Ohio seemed to know the story.)

Our pediatrician was, as usual, unconcerned. "You have to realize that children develop at their own pace," he told me. "He's a little late talking but it will come—maybe you're giving him everything he wants and he doesn't *have* to talk! Look at him—he's a big, strong boy. Be patient!"

Then Sean developed a passion that made all his other fixations seem mild by comparison—chains. The garage behind our house had double-windowed wooden doors that pulled open from the center. Each door was attached to the garage by a heavy chain. Sean would find a long stick or a broom or shovel handle, snag the chains, one after the other, pulling each as high as he could, then let go. He'd back up into the driveway and watch them swing, giggling. He did it over and over, hundreds of times,

30

never tiring of the activity. After a week or so, he redefined the game. He got both chains swinging, then he turned and dashed into the house, where he hoisted himself up on the kitchen counter so that he could watch the swinging chains through the window. He never took his eyes off them until they were still. If I happened to be standing at the sink, he elbowed and pushed me away, rather as if I were clothes hanging on a line.

Later he extended his range—he'd swing the chains, tear into the house, roar through the kitchen, and gallop up the stairs to the second floor window, where he'd stand until the chains had stopped moving. If I was in his path when he came through the kitchen, he never saw me; if I didn't jump out of his way, he ran into me and kept going; if I held onto him he became hysterical, like a trapped animal, screaming and fighting to get loose. He had to get to the top of the stairs before the chains stopped; nothing else in his life mattered.

One night after dinner the four of us went to the grocery store. Sean was walking ahead of Ron as we passed the people in line at the check-out counter. Suddenly I noticed an elderly woman who was wearing glasses around her neck on a chain. I turned quickly to Sean but he was already gone, forcing his way through the people in front of her. He reached up, his hand closing around the chain, ready to give it a good swing. I lunged for him and grabbed his hand, the shocked eyes of the old woman peering at me over his head. I pried his fingers loose, apologizing, smiling at the woman—as if it were a perfectly ordinary misunderstanding—before I dragged him away.

One of my favorite things was chains; I loved the texture of chains. Each link looked the same and even felt the same as all the others.

31

Because the chains on our garage were too high for me to reach, they were very mysterious to me—I wanted so much to touch them, but I had to use a stick instead. Since I couldn't reach them with my hands, I made them swing. I really loved the repetition of the swinging movement—I wanted to see the chains from all different heights and angles. The more I saw them swing, the more entranced I became, and the more I wanted to do nothing but watch them. It was what I loved. It was my routine. My mother kept trying to interrupt me, but that never stopped me.

Every day Sean returned to the garage doors. We tried to divert him, but as always, nothing worked. Then Ron came up with a brilliant idea—he made Sean a replica of our garage for Christmas. It was wonderful, made of wood, with real chains on doors that actually opened and a roof that lifted off to serve as a large toy box—it was perfect! Sean never touched it. He got a broom and went back to the garage outside.

Then he broke a windowpane—he hit the glass with the chain so hard that the glass shattered. We realized that we had to put a stop to this game of his for good. We swept up the glass and Ron replaced the pane. We explained that he could not play with the chains anymore, that the glass could break and he could hurt himself.

We gave him other toys—surely, we thought, he was old enough now to begin taking an interest in real toys. We tried getting him to play games with us. But as soon as we turned our backs he was out hitting the chains with a stick. Before I could get to him, another window was broken.

We realized there was no point in trying to reason with Sean, so we bought a padlock and Ron replaced the second broken window. When he was through he put the lock on the doors and fastened it securely. It was over. An hour later I looked up from putting away groceries in the kitchen when I heard the sound of breaking glass. Sean stood in the driveway giggling. In his hand was a long board from which hung the brand-new padlock, still locked, and a metal plate. He was watching the chains swing. I did the only thing I could do—I got my camera and took his picture.

The only time our son slowed down was when he was sick, a rare but startling occurrence. When he had a fever or an upset stomach he'd allow me to put him to bed, and I'd sit with him, rubbing his back, stroking his head. He accepted the attention, sometimes reaching out to take my hand. I read him stories, talked to him, told him over and over that I loved him. When he looked at me his eyes, though dulled, were without fear; sometimes he stared at me for a long time as if trying to remember who I was. He was like another child altogether. *This is my son*, I thought, this sweet, angelic little boy, free of the frenzied behavior that drives him.

He was pliant, vulnerable for the day or two the illness lasted, and his recovery was always the same—instantaneous. I'd leave his room to get him some broth and I'd return to find an empty bed, Sean crouched on the floor flinging toys off his desk, his eyes hooded, his behavior back to full speed.

He had an unusually high tolerance for pain. He barely responded when he fell and cut himself or even when he burned his hand. We had an expandable wooden gate across the top of the cellar stairs to keep him from going down there alone, but one day he flung himself at the gate and crashed through it. His body flew through the air and over the stairs, and he landed with a nauseating thud on the concrete floor below. I screamed, sure he was dead, and Ron and I ran to pick him up. He was giggling, slightly dazed, one arm bent at a horrible angle. We rushed him to the hospital, where the broken arm was set; there was no injury to his head nor even a bruise on any other part of his body. Throughout the time we were at the hospital, Sean never cried.

We brought him home with his arm in a heavy white cast. He went into the bathroom and pointed at the sink. I filled a glass of water for him to drink, and when I handed it to him, he sat on the edge of the bathtub and flipped himself over backwards, crashing into the tub. He lay there giggling until we pulled him out, sure that his arm had been damaged. He shook us off and ran to his room—business as usual.

The one thing that did hurt him was having his scalp touched; when I washed his hair he squirmed and cried out, trying to push my hands away. Though I was as gentle as possible, it was obviously painful to him. It was even worse when I brushed his hair—he screamed *"ow!"* over and over, wrenching away from me. What could be causing the pain? His scalp was perfectly healthy, I used the softest brush I could find. The pediatrician, when I asked, said, "Hmmm, I don't think it's really hurting him—a lot of kids just don't like to have their hair washed or combed."

Almost without realizing it, I had become more and more isolated in the almost four years since Sean's birth. I couldn't even remember the last time a friend had been in the house. It was so much easier not to invite people than to put up with the strain and acute embarrassment of our son's behavior. Ron and I went out when we could, though on his teacher's salary we had little money left over for entertainment. Most of the time when we did go out, my parents watched the children; they never made us feel we were asking too much, that we were inconveniencing them. Baby-sitters were a problem, not only because we couldn't afford them but also because after their first experience with Sean, they usually refused to return.

The idea of looking for a job never seriously occurred to me. It was the sixties, and we were living in Ohio, in a small community of white, middle-class people; I didn't know a single working woman who was also the mother of preschool children. Once, in desperation, I mentioned to my mother that I'd love to get out of the house and work. She looked at me, shocked. "How can you even *think* something like that when you have the responsibility of two children at home?!" It was as if I'd suggested becoming a call girl.

So I read hundreds of books, I cleaned, I baked all our bread like some pioneer woman of the last century. When Ron came home at night I waited for him to praise the newly washed windows or the sparkling floors or the fresh sheets. If he didn't, I was deeply disappointed. After all, I'd worked hard all day in spite of Sean's behavior. Couldn't Ron at least *notice?*

I barely gave him time to get inside the house in the evenings before I told him how the day had gone—Sean's recalcitrance, his disregard of anything that got in his way, the bizarre things he had done. I cataloged my frustration, my sense of futility. I fell into dark moods; life was slipping past while I did nothing but yell, hit, fail at motherhood. Ron was always supportive, good-humored; he listened to all of it without cutting me off. But, I thought, why shouldn't he be upbeat, positive? He left the house every day, had a job for which he received a paycheck, talked to real people, adults. I couldn't remember what it was like to have a conversation with another grown-up—the very notion had begun to frighten me. Ron was actually doing something—*living*—and others responded to him. He was a good teacher, he was effective, his students liked him, while I . . . I was a terrible mother.

In school I had always been known for level-headedness, calmness in the face of crisis. In high school, for God's sake, I had been voted the one with the best sense of humor. But I wasn't laughing anymore. Nor was I logical, level-headed, or unemotional. I existed in an emotional state that ranged from furious to enraged. I smacked Sean with a wooden spoon to save the blood vessels in my hands; I began by tapping him lightly on the behind, but the taps had no effect, so they got harder, until sometimes I hit him as hard as I could. Even so, he scarcely seemed to notice, hardly responding to the pain I knew I must be causing.

When I spoke to him in a normal voice he ignored me completely, as if human speech were below his level of comprehension, so I got louder and louder, until I was shouting all the time, trying desperately to get through to him. I was now a mother who responded to her son's behavior with physical and verbal abuse.

I, and Ron, had to get help. Sean was not improving and we were desperate. "It doesn't matter if your family doesn't want to talk about it," Ron said. "We've got to find somebody who does, who can help us."

"I was so sure he'd grow out of all this," I said, trying to smile. "What if we find out it's even worse than we think?"

"Then at least we'll know what we're dealing with."

I nodded.

"I'll ask somebody at school for a recommendation tomorrow. We'll find someone, don't worry."

Ron spoke with a friend who was a guidance counselor at his school. We were referred to a psychologist with a reputation for being good with children. Without saying anything to our families, we made an appointment for a consultation.

He was waiting for us in an empty classroom with huge wooden windows. An old-fashioned "cloak room" with four doors covered the rear wall. Sean, without a glance at the psychologist, headed immediately for the doors, pulling them open, slamming them shut. Then he climbed onto a desk and tried to reach the cupboards above them, whining when they were too high. Ron ran to get him before he fell. The psychologist, Dr. Cohen, tried to carry on a conversation with us in spite of the fact that Sean had gone back to opening and slamming the huge doors, and most of what he said was drowned out. He asked us a lot of questions—the circumstances of Sean's birth, my medical history—but we could barely hear him. Ron and I took turns trying to get Sean to sit down, to come and meet the man who wanted to talk with him a little. Finally Ron managed to get Sean to sit at a desk; Dr. Cohen asked him questions but there was no response. We explained that Sean could not yet talk, a fact that had already been explained when we spoke to him by phone.

The doctor put some papers in front of our son, who moved them around the desk but didn't look at them. "Sean, point to the car," the doctor said. Nothing. He repeated the instruction. He tried another object, but still no response. He was persistent, though, and after a number of repetitions Sean reluctantly pointed to a few of the pictures. He seemed bored, unwilling to do what he was asked, I thought, rather than unable to.

Cohen made his diagnosis on the spot and in front of Sean. "He is definitely of dull-normal intelligence," he said. "He's not really retarded, but he will never be a good student, either; everything will always be hard for him, but he is what we call 'educable.'" He turned to me. "How old was Sean when you had your second child?"

"Just under two—twenty-three months."

He nodded knowingly. "The worst possible time to have another child," he said sadly. "You see, between eighteen months and two years is the worst age for the older child." I looked at him. How many people have babies when I did?— surely millions! But no one I'd heard of had one who behaved like ours.

He had more to say. "Sean, come here." Sean did, slowly and reluctantly, avoiding eye contact with the doctor. Cohen knelt down and put his arm around Sean's waist, speaking into his face—as close as he could get with Sean squirming uncomfortably. He asked more questions: What do you like to do, Sean?

Do you have a baby sister? Do you like to play outside? Sean looked at him for a moment, puzzled, then twisted away, back to the cloak-room doors.

The psychologist stood up, dusting off his knees. "You see how much better he responds when you put yourself on his level," he said. Ron and I looked at each other blankly. "Do you realize," he continued, "how much taller you are than he is? Imagine how it feels to him when he has to constantly look up at you when you speak to him! If you simply kneel down when you address him he won't feel dwarfed by your size!"

Could this *be*? My first impulse was to burst into laughter. At once I was filled with remorse, with guilt. Why hadn't we seen it ourselves?—such an obvious thing. We drove home in a daze, not knowing whether to laugh or cry. Dull-normal. They were chilling words but described a condition we would have to accept. Everything would always be difficult for our son, and, as if that weren't bad enough, we had probably ruined him by having Megan at exactly the wrong time.

There was a bunch of identical doors in the room. I needed to know where those doors went—did they end or did they lead somewhere else? I felt better as soon as I saw the doors; before that I was uncomfortable because my routine had been broken by coming to this place.

Once I began opening and closing all the doors, I was all right. Of course, I had to keep doing it because even if I saw where one door went, I thought it might change, so I had to open it again and again to check. I had to do that with all of them because I could never be sure unless I did.

A man was in the room with me but I don't know who it was.

Once he got down on the floor beside me—I was very shocked that he would do such a thing. I still don't know what he was doing. I was so surprised by his action that I remember actually looking at him.

Since Ron's teacher's salary didn't cover our modest living expenses, he took a part-time job as a television director, working every weekend from 4:00 P.M. until 1:00 in the morning. He also often had to do extra school duties, without extra pay—selling popcorn at sports events, chaperoning dances, directing plays. On weekday evenings he attended classes at the university where he was working on a degree in education—a requirement for teaching in the public schools, where his Bachelor of Fine Arts was not acceptable. The kids and I were alone together almost all the time, and a single day with Sean felt like an eternity.

I thought I was drowning. On many days, sometimes for weeks on end, I had no sense of reality. I became absent-minded, unable to finish anything I started.

Sean had become clearly jealous of Megan. He invaded her room, ripped up her drawings, threw her toys out the window, dumped blocks and Tinker Toys into her closet. Why wouldn't he be jealous? After all, she could do things he couldn't do, and we never yelled at her. She was praised; he was punished. I was sympathetic to the reasons but enraged at the result.

I watched the clock until Ron finally came home. If he had a free evening we often went for a drive through the park for a change of scene or, if we had the money, we'd all have dinner out. Our favorite place to go was a big, noisy, farm restaurant.

The food was awful, the atmosphere nonexistent, but it had one irresistible feature—one of the tables sat under an enormous air-conditioner in the corner; the thing made such a racket that no one else would sit there, but it was "our table," where Sean's kicking and yelling were nearly inaudible.

We looked forward to spring and summer like prisoners promised a reprieve. Ron built a wonderful playhouse for the kids in the yard, with a sliding board roof. Megan loved it—it was her own house, her airplane, or her boat. While she played happily in the little house or swam in her plastic pool, Sean threw everything he could pick up into a tree in the middle of the yard. Mostly he chose his own toys to throw, and unless it was heavy enough to cause real damage when it fell out of the tree onto one of our heads, I was content to let him fling whatever he wanted into the branches. As always, he was alone in the world and, if no one interfered with him, he would play his game for hours at a time.

Trouble arose when all his toys were gone, stuck somewhere above our heads, and he began using Megan's toys, ripped from her hands and hurled into the tree. When there was nothing left to throw he wailed, staring above him with his hands up.

Then Ron and I began having this conversation a lot:

HE: Did you use my wrench for something?
SHE: No, why?
HE: Because I know I put it on the shelf in the cellar and it's not there.
SHE: Well, I didn't take it.
HE: Are you sure?

I couldn't find my screwdriver, the corkscrew, and the kitchen tongs. Ron lost a hammer, a bedroom slipper, neckties, and shoehorns. In the fall, after the leaves had all fallen from the tree in the yard, we found everything. Ron and I stood beneath its bare branches—well, not bare exactly—and stared upward. There was a serving spoon, an oven glove, a shoe, several towels, a ruler, a light bulb still in its box, the egg beater, a thermometer, sponges, a scarf . . . strange fruit. We stood shoulder to shoulder, pointing out things we hadn't seen in months—two aerial archaeologists.

In time we discovered that Sean had an indoor version of this game as well. We both bought him toys with such high hopes, always with the idea that "this is something he does relentlessly, so maybe he'll play with a toy that does almost the same thing but isn't dangerous!" It never worked. Most of the things in his room were broken, many toys just disappeared. When I trimmed the bushes beneath his bedroom window the following spring, I found the toys. He had loosened one of his screens and thrown the toys out the window to watch them fall.

Tinker Toys were an ongoing problem. We had been so sure he would like them—and he did, in a way. Sometimes, if Ron or I sat with him, he helped us build a structure for a minute or two; almost at once, though, he would begin rolling the pieces off the table. When he got his hands on a whole box of them, he took off the lid and flung them into his closet. I'd make him pick them up, then take them away. Megan had a set as well, however, so he would immediately just take hers instead and throw those into his closet. I'd find him leaning against his closet door, listening intently. It was clear that, as with most things he did, his activities "meant" something to him, though I couldn't even imagine what he was doing. He never tried to hide his actions, and he always responded with fury or frustration when he was stopped.

This child was Ron's and mine; he looked like both of us. Yet, although we had spent more than four years together, he was a complete stranger to us. We never knew what he was doing, what he was thinking. The fact that he didn't talk was more and more frightening—he still pointed and grunted, usually with great impatience, when he wanted something. I had begun to wonder if he was from another planet.

I got enormous pleasure from throwing things into a big tree in our backyard. It didn't matter to me what shape or size the object was—I took toys out of the sandbox or things from the kitchen (if I could sneak in and grab something) and threw them all into the tree. I wanted to see how high they would go and where they would get caught. I loved the pattern: throwing the object as high as I could, seeing where it hit the tree, following its downward movement with my eyes, and watching where it got stuck. Sometimes, though, I'd look away after I made the throw and just listen to the sound it made as it fell rustling through the leaves and branches. I loved doing this so much that I kept throwing the same thing into the tree over and over until it stayed there, even if it took forever. While I was doing it I had no sense of time—hours passed but I didn't notice. When Mom saw me playing this game and tried to stop me, I got really furious with her and thought, "How dare she keep me from doing what I want to do!" It gave me a feeling of security and a lot of pleasure no matter how much I did it. I wasn't trying to hurt anyone; I was in my own world, and whatever else went on nearby, I was not aware of it.

44

When Mom called me I would suddenly get scared because I knew I would be yelled at once again for doing something I enjoyed. This was my world and I was in control—I controlled the object; it went up into the tree because I made it do so—and if the thing I was throwing belonged to somebody else, it didn't matter to me or even have anything to do with me. When I got yelled at or punished, I felt as if I were being invaded; I was no longer in control—someone had control over me again.

Tinker Toys were one of my favorites. I'd take the whole box of them, open my closet door, and throw them in, slamming the door shut as fast as I could. I believed that the inside of my closet was whirling around like a washing machine, spinning the Tinker Toys. I could never see it happening, though, because when I opened the door the spinning would stop, just as it did when I opened the washing-machine door. But I knew what was going on in there.

I pleaded with Sean's pediatrician for advice. Where could we take him for help? He suggested, somewhat reluctantly, the Speech and Hearing Center. I made an appointment. After spending a scant half hour with Sean the therapist said, "This is definitely *not* a speech problem we have here—there's really nothing we can do for him. If I were you, though, I would take him to see a neurologist." Seeing my expression she said, "It may not be a neurological problem at all, but it's a place to start, anyway."

She recommended a doctor. He was, she said, the best in town. We had to wait three long, anxious weeks for the appointment. A neurologist? What did the speech therapist think was wrong, and why had I been afraid to ask her at the time?

The fee to see this doctor was a staggering $100, and we simply didn't have it. But if he could find the cause of Sean's problems it would be well worth it. We borrowed the money.

We walked into the office, Ron holding one of Sean's hands, I the other. The receptionist looked surprised to see us. "Oh," she said, "Doctor is due at the hospital in half an hour— something has come up. He had to cut your time short, to fifteen minutes at most—I hope that will be all right." Ron had taken the afternoon off; we had worried about this appointment for three weeks. We couldn't stand to postpone it until the next opening—four weeks away, she said proudly. But why hadn't she phoned us? She had been busy, she said, but told us, "You can still see Doctor today—just be brief."

She ushered us in. Ron and I sat in the two straight chairs facing the desk and the doctor who sat behind it, a gray-haired man with deeply etched lines in a stern—if not cruel—face. Sean twisted away from Ron and made a dash into the adjoining bathroom. The doctor frowned. "What's he doing in there?"

Ron went to find out. Sean was standing on the back of the toilet, stretching up as far as he could to reach the cord on the blind that covered the window. The cord was swinging wildly. Ron carried Sean, who protested with a yell, back into the office and held him, writhing, on his lap.

The doctor asked me questions. He seemed angry with me, impatient if I hesitated before answering. He asked about my pregnancy, Sean's birth. There was nothing to tell: no drugs, no alcohol, no cigarettes, no illness. I had been tired for nine months, that was all. I hadn't even taken aspirin.

"The first thing we have to do is have him take a neumoencephalogram—then we'll go from there." He stood up, looking at his watch. "My nurse will schedule it."

"Wait," I said as he headed for his office door. "We don't want to do that to him—I've read that people often get terrible headaches from it and that the results are often wrong anyway." (I had been reading everything I could find since we had made the appointment.)

He looked at me with undisguised fury. "You came to me for my opinion and now you have it. If you don't follow my recommendation, I'm not responsible for the results. This is a very abnormal child."

"But isn't there an alternative to a neumoencephalogram?"

"Yes, find another doctor," he said. "I'm a very busy man."

He ushered us out. It had taken exactly eight minutes. It had cost $100.

We went back to our guidance-counselor friend. There had to be somebody, we pleaded, who could help us, give us some answers, some reasons, tell us how to get through to our child before we wasted any more time. We got another recommendation. Dr. Logan, our friend said, was a neurological pediatrician, one of only five in the country. He should be able to tell us what was wrong and refer us to whatever kind of help Sean needed. He was expensive, but worth it; also, he was in Akron, Ohio—a city sixty miles away, to which neither Ron nor I had ever been. Unfortunately, there was just no one in the immediate area he could recommend.

Our appointment this time was on a Saturday morning. We drove in silence, both Ron and I filled with apprehension. We found the address and parked. The building was constructed in the fifties, a cheerless structure of concrete slabs and insipid yellow aluminum panels. We went in. The office had a small waiting room with a receptionist. There were two other children and their mothers, also waiting. I looked at the children closely. What was wrong with them? One seemed retarded, the other quite "normal" and well behaved.

When it was our turn the receptionist said that Ron and I were to meet with the doctor alone, that Sean was to remain with her until he was called for. We looked at her. She was sitting at her desk, dressed immaculately, every hair sprayed into place. Was that the kind of kids they saw here?—kids who would sit in a waiting room without their parents? I wanted to warn her but didn't know what to say. Ron was explaining to Sean what was happening—that we'd be right inside the door and that in a few minutes he would come in with us, but that for now he would wait with the woman at the desk. Sean rocked on his chair, swinging his feet vigorously, looking everywhere but at Ron.

We went in and the receptionist closed the door behind us. The doctor stood up to shake hands. He was a stocky man, younger than I had imagined. We sat down facing him and he folded his arms across his chest. He looked at us for a moment in silence and then began asking questions, all directed at me. He never took his eyes from my face; he made no notes.

"Now, mother," he began, "tell me about your son."

Mother? . . . Where to begin? I tried to explain what Sean's behavior was like; I faltered. I found myself making excuses for what he did. Sean began to yell in the waiting room. He pounded on the closed—and, we now saw locked—door, trying to open it. When he couldn't, he started to kick it. We could hear the receptionist trying to pull him away. Still the doctor watched me.

Ron started to get to his feet. Without taking his eyes from mine, Dr. Logan waved one hand dismissively at the door. "Leave him," he said. "Go on, mother."

"Excuse me," I said, trying to smile, "but I'm not your mother—my name is Judy." His eyes changed slightly; there was a pause.

"I see we're having trouble accepting the role of motherhood."

"No—not at all. It's just that I'm Sean's mother, not yours." To soften the words I smiled, hopefully. His face remained impassive.

More than anything, I wanted to fling myself across that desk and slug him, to knock some expression onto that blank face. But there was something stuck in my chest. Was he right? Could he see something I was trying to hide from myself? Ron took my hand and squeezed it, hard. He began to explain what it was like to live with Sean. His description was clear; he chose just the right incidents to point out the problems.

Dr. Logan didn't look at him. He interrupted Ron with more questions for me. I was deafened by the noise Sean was making; I could scarcely think. I was numb with embarrassment, half expecting that all three of us would be thrown out of the office and asked never to return. I talked on, hardly listening to what I was saying but aware that I was again minimizing Sean's behavior aberrations. I was soaked in sweat, my back stuck fast to the wooden chair. I knew suddenly that at the end of all this Dr. Logan would say, "It's not his fault—it's *yours*! You're not a good mother and you've even ruined my chair!"

"How are you getting all this?" I asked, to shift the focus off myself. "You're not writing anything down."

"I don't have to write anything," he said. "I remember everything I hear that's important."

I sneaked a glance at the door. At any moment, I feared, it would be shattered—Sean appearing in a gaping hole in the center, a jagged board in his hand.

At last the questions were over. "You may let Sean in now," Dr. Logan said. Ron opened the door and Sean catapulted into the office, his face crimson, still yelling. In the background I saw the receptionist trying to adjust her clothes, her hair tangled and undone. She averted her head and closed the door.

"Sean, come with me." Dr. Logan took our son firmly by the arm as Sean pulled back, twisting and yelling, his face sweaty. "I'm going to examine him in here," the doctor said over his shoulder as he dragged Sean into an adjoining room and closed the door behind them. Ron and I looked at each other. Frankenstein's laboratory.

Fifteen minutes passed, in silence, then Dr. Logan reappeared. "Follow me, please." We went into a dark room with an examining table and a child-sized blackboard on a tripod. Sean looked disoriented, his face smeared with tears, his hair plastered to his head. I put my arms around him. What must he think was happening to him?

"His reflexes are normal," Dr. Logan began brusquely. "I gave him a medical exam and I see nothing abnormal physically. But I want him to have an EEG at Children's Hospital. I'll set that up. Now, Sean, I want you to do something for me."

He handed Sean a piece of chalk. "Draw me an X on the blackboard." Sean didn't move. Logan turned him toward the board. "Here, look. Draw this." He made a large X with the chalk. "Go ahead, Sean—you make one like that."

Sean drew a shaky line. "Finish it—like this," the doctor said. He drew a second X. Sean made another line, not intersecting the first.

"Okay. Now, do this." Logan drew a circle; Sean made an irregularly curved line. The doctor tried more geometric shapes, but Sean dropped the chalk and refused to do any more.

"I want him to have the EEG before I see you next—I need the results before I can give you a diagnosis. We'll do it a week from today, and the following week you'll come back here. We should know something by then."

We drove home shaken and confused. Sean was more subdued than we had ever seen him. Neither of us liked Logan, but should that matter? If he could offer help, we'd take it—after all, who else *was* there? And an EEG was harmless—no headache, even if the results were often inconclusive. At least he hadn't recommended a neumoencephalogram.

The following week we were at the Children's Hospital at 9:00 A.M. We explained to Sean as much as we could what the process would be. He fought being put onto the table, but the nurses were kind and effective. He relaxed almost at once as they affixed the electrodes to his head. I was on the verge of throwing up and must have looked it. One of the nurses smiled and patted my arm. "Don't worry—he won't feel anything and he'll probably sleep through it."

Oh sure, I thought. She doesn't know my child! But she was right—Sean fell asleep at once and barely woke up as Ron lifted him from the table and carried him to the car. We hugged him, smiling with relief, and told him what a good boy he had been—he had looked just like a spaceman! (Did he have any idea what a spaceman was?)

The following Saturday we were back at Dr. Logan's office. He saw all three of us at once. Nothing had shown up on the EEG, he said, but he hadn't expected it would. He suspected minimal brain damage. "However, what we've got here, I'm afraid, is a case of autism."

Autism? We had never heard the word before.

"It's a dysfunction of the brain," he explained. "He was obviously born with it. No one knows what causes it or even what it is, really—and there is no cure as such. He has an inability to communicate properly—it has nothing to do with his intelligence; he could be very bright. The trouble is, with autism, you have the basic dysfunction, then on top of that are all the psychological problems that result from the dysfunction."

So it had a name. There was a medical reason. This man knew of other children like Sean, other families who lived the way we did. A hard kernel of pain inside my chest opened, and I was flooded with relief. Maybe it wasn't me after all!

"But what can we do?" Ron asked.

First, we were to give him medication, Ritalin, to control his hyperactivity. "You have to calm him down so you can at least get through to him as much as possible," Logan said. In addition, we were to see a clinical psychologist, also in Akron, once a month. He would give us a program to follow, designed around Sean's particular needs. We could, in fact, go to his office today, meet him, and set up a schedule.

"Since Sean is only a year away from kindergarten, there's no time to waste—he could never go to school in his present condition!" Dr. Logan wrote us a prescription and gave us directions.

We went immediately to meet Dr. Rossi. His office was in an old Victorian house shrouded in bushes. Inside, the rooms were shabby, the furnishings worn and neglected. Rossi was a tall man with a heavy black beard and fierce dark eyes. Once again we went through a description of Sean's behavior, our problems in dealing with him. He talked to Sean, asked him to draw, to walk in different directions while he watched him intently.

I was very frightened of Dr. Rossi. I was intimidated, even before I met him, by the outside of his house. It was three stories high, and it made me squeamish and uncomfortable—it looked secretive and strange, and there were tall bushes surrounding it. I had a very strong feeling—I did not want to be there—and I felt it as soon as I stepped out of the car. I did not belong here in this funny house; it was outside my world. I carried those feelings with me as I was made to enter the place.

My fear got worse when I saw Dr. Rossi. What scared me most was his bushy beard, and the fact that it was a dark beard bothered me too. He had a lot of dark features, in fact—his voice, his hair, his skin color, and his clothes. All of these things made me uneasy, but it was the beard that was the focus of my fear. I felt threatened by men who wore beards, so later I hated it when my dad grew one; it took me a long time to accept it, though I never told Dad how I felt.

Now, with Dr. Rossi, my fear and discomfort made me less than optimistic about being in this house. I was being examined by this man for God knows what reason—after all, I felt fine, I wasn't sick! Just the way he looked at me made me think that he could not only exert control over me but that he also had the potential to hurt me physically. To me, dark people like him were always threatening—not black people, but those with dark olive skin and black hair.

I did not want to go into his office, both because I was afraid

of him and because being there made me feel there was some-
thing wrong with me. Not only was I constantly being punished
at home for things that gave me pleasure, but now some stranger
was treating me as if he, too, thought I was "bad" for some
reason.

He told me to do things. He wanted me to draw a house—
a square with a triangle for a roof. I heard what he said, but
I didn't understand that the square and the triangle should be
connected. I drew them separately. He said I hadn't done it the
way he asked, so I got frustrated and gave up trying. I pretended
that I was in my own world—that was the only way I knew to
remove myself from this situation that I didn't want to be in.
Now it was okay—I could hear him but without letting him get
through.

We said that Sean's perception of himself appeared to be that of
a cardboard cutout—he didn't realize that there was a back or
sides to his body. He washed only the front of his face—when
we could get him to do even that—the very front of his hair,
one side of his hands. He couldn't dress himself; he tried to put
his shirt on like a straitjacket, holding it in front of him. He
couldn't tell the difference between the front and back of his
pants and usually tried to put them on upside down. Buttons
and shoelaces were impossible. He never made any attempt to
dress himself unless I forced him to, just as he had not tried to
feed himself until I had worked with him over and over, encour-
againg him to pick up the spoon and do it himself. He seemed
terrified of failure—if something didn't go well once, he would
often not try it a second time. When he used crayons, his hand
movements were from right to left, bottom to top.

Sean needed, Rossi said, to be put on a retraining program at once. All his movements had to be reversed, many of his perceptions altered. It was going to take half an hour every day, and I was to do it with him—if Ron and I both got involved, Sean would be hopelessly confused. The materials were simple and inexpensive. He showed me exactly what to do.

I wasted no time. Here was something I could *do*, something that would help Sean, at last! The next day I got everything ready. I made sandpaper letters and shapes, which Sean would trace with his fingers over and over, the way he would eventually learn to print them. I bought beanbags and a bucket for him to toss them into, clothespins and a round wastebasket for him to clip them onto, a pegboard and golf tees, a sheet of heavy acetate, new crayons. We got his prescription filled and gave him the first capsules. I was ready to begin.

First, the coordination exercises. While Megan took her nap in the afternoon, Sean and I went upstairs to his room. I gave him a hug and told him that we were going to play some games that he would like. I gave him one of the beanbags and showed him the bucket a few feet away. "Now, throw the beanbag into the bucket—like this." I demonstrated. He dropped the bean-bag on the floor and threw himself down. I picked him up and hugged him again. I repeated the instructions, with the same result. "Take it slowly," Dr. Rossi had cautioned. I tried once more, then switched to another activity.

"Look, Sean—" I pointed out the clothespins that I had painted in bright primary colors. I showed him how they opened and closed. "Let's put some on this basket," I said, clipping several to the edge of the wastebasket. "See?" I handed him one and he dropped it. I picked it up and gave it to him again. He set it on the table and flicked it off. I picked it up.

"No, don't do that. Put it on here." (I was to tell him: "Put two red pins on, now put three yellow pins, now one blue one." He was to do what I said. But it wasn't working that way, and I knew I was expecting too much too soon.)

I sat down at his little table and showed him the acetate sheet and crayons. Taking his arm, I pulled him into the chair next to me. I placed a simple drawing of a house under the acetate, then asked him to draw it, putting his hand with the crayon on top of the drawing. He made a long line down the clear plastic. I took his hand and traced the shape with him once, then a second time. "See, honey—just do it like this—draw the house." I let go and he threw himself off the chair and onto the floor.

Dr. Rossi's voice spoke inside my head: "Don't rush him—let him go at his own pace." I decided we'd had enough for the first day.

But the second day was the same, and the third. Sean was hostile, uncooperative, restless, bored, disruptive. Or he simply couldn't do any of the things I was asking him to do because they were beyond his capacity. I didn't know whether to keep trying or to quit. It seemed as if I were making him more frustrated than ever. I called Dr. Rossi.

"Keep at it; don't give up," he said. "Just be patient with him and he'll get it in time."

Sean and I faced the retraining exercises every afternoon. It was awful. I knew he could do some of the tasks, but he refused to try. I tried to use Megan's nap time to work with Sean, but sometimes when she couldn't sleep she came into his room with us. She'd watch for a minute or two, then try to help. "Look, I'll play too—see, Sean, like this!" and she'd toss a beanbag into the can. She was gentle with him, as if at not quite three she were an older child helping a younger one. "He doesn't understand just yet," she'd say as he twisted away, covering his face with his hands so he couldn't see his sister.

The Ritalin did have an effect on Sean's behavior; for four days he was quieter, less hysterical. On the fifth day he was back to full speed. At the end of the week I called Dr. Logan. "Increase the dosage," he said. "Sometimes an amount that would put an adult like you or me to sleep has no effect on these kids." Uneasily, we did what he said. A calming effect was apparent for almost a week, then it, too, wore off. Dr. Logan advised us to continue giving him the medicine; if we didn't, he said, Sean's hyperactivity would increase.

I tried everything to get him to throw the beanbags, to clip on the clothespins, to put the golf tees into the pegboard. Should I force him? Wasn't I clearly reinforcing his "bad" behavior if I didn't? I began to insist. "Sean, draw this right now!" My voice grew louder, I spoke through clenched teeth. I became desperate. If these exercises really could help him, improve his coordination, correct his perspective, then he *had* to do them. Otherwise he would never be able to go to school next year, and then what? But it had to be fun, a game, no pressure. It *had* to be *fun*!

Another day, a fresh start. No pressure. "Honey, let's trace this letter A with our fingers." Sean stared at the closet. "Come on, trace this letter A." Nope, no dice. He giggled, twisting and squirming. I grabbed him and made him sit still. "Sean, do this right now!" No reaction. I began to yell, then to cry.

By this time we had told my parents about our trip to Akron, the diagnosis, the exercises. They had listened in silence and looked sympathetic but had asked only one question. "Why," my mother said sadly, "are you doing this?" (Inventing his problems? Not understanding him? Not loving him? Punishing my child for my inability to be a good mother?) "Why?" I said. "Because we're desperate. Sean's not a normal child and we need help!" She shook her head sadly and walked away.

Our son was almost five years old. Except for a few words, he still couldn't talk, he did whatever he wanted to do, and wouldn't listen to me or to Ron. All he seemed to want was to be left alone to do every bizarre thing he could think of. In one year we hoped to send him to school where he'd be expected to sit at a desk in a room full of kids and pay attention to the teacher. My God.

At home Mom tried to get me to do the exercises Dr. Rossi had given her. I hated doing the things she told me to—they were boring and not at all what I wanted to do. What I did want was to be free, to do the repetitious games I made up for myself. After all, I couldn't fail with the things I chose. If I did what my mother wanted, there was the possibility that I would fail, not perform well, and I knew what would happen then. I got very frustrated and angry.

I was aware that Mom got upset when I refused to do what she wanted, but I was so focused on my own behavior that I had no idea what she was upset about. Her reactions only confused me.

"It's impossible! It's not working and I can't do it!" I was on the verge of tears. "He won't try, no matter what I do, no matter how patient I am. Then I get so angry with him that I start yelling at him—the whole thing is doing more harm than good!"

"You *cannot* get angry with him," Dr. Rossi said firmly.

"You've got to be more patient and keep trying. All of this is hard for him, remember."

It was our first monthly visit to Akron; I had four weeks of failure and frustration bottled up inside me. "But what else can I do?" I asked. "He constantly repeats the behaviors we can't allow—it's destructive and hypnotic. Everything he does is bizarre, and if I ignore it he gets worse and worse. To stop him I have to scream and punish him, and then I can't stand my *own* behavior!"

"You must stop responding negatively to everything he does and start reinforcing his good behavior. Praise him every time he does something positive, no matter what it is—even little things. By now he has a terrible self-image, so you've got to do everything you can to build up his good feelings about himself."

I couldn't agree more! Such common sense. But *what* good behavior? Didn't anyone listen to me? There wasn't any good behavior! No neutral behavior! We weren't stupid and we weren't cruel—wouldn't we praise him to the skies if we could find anything to praise? I was furious that this man could be so insensitive to the real situation. Then, a moment later, I realized that Rossi was giving me good advice, saying the only things he could say. No doubt, I said to myself, he believes I've exaggerated Sean's behavior, that because I'm so angry with him I've painted a bleaker picture than the truth. Probably, I thought, most parents would react that way. And then I wondered: *Is* that what I'm doing?

Rossi worked with Sean a while, giving him the directions I had tried so unsuccessfully. He spoke sharply, fixing Sean with those intense eyes. Sean looked unsettled; he wasn't used to being spoken to like this by a dark-bearded stranger. Rossi was giving him movement instructions: walk forward one step, raise one arm. Sean responded; he took a step, lifted his right arm. Then he'd had enough and flung himself across the room on his knees.

Rossi turned to me. "You see, he *can* do it. You have to be patient but firm and keep working at it."

I drove home filled with determination. I had decided that the half-hour sessions were too long, that we'd do two fifteen-minute ones instead. I was patient, most of the time, and we kept at it. I played games with my mind, telling myself I was in a movie, acting the role of a wonderful mother whose patience was eternal—a real Annie Sullivan. This was just a job, I told myself—I had no emotional stake in any of this.

At the end of the week there was a breakthrough. "Sean, throw the beanbag into the can." He did. I froze, staring at the can with the beanbag in it. Then I looked at Sean. "You did it!" I yelled, grabbing him and hugging him to me, my eyes filling with tears. He picked up another one and threw that in. He threw a third and the can fell over. He laughed—not the strange giggle that wove through our lives, but a real laugh. Drunk with success I began to combine the other directions: Take two steps back, then throw it. He did! Take one step forward and throw. He did it again!

I told Megan about what Sean had done, how much fun we had had. She laughed happily, clapped her hands. When Ron came home he heard it all. Thrilled, he picked Sean up and whirled him around, hugging him.

The next day it was as if it had never happened. Sean acted as if he had never set eyes on the beanbags before, as if he had no idea what I meant when I said, "Take two steps backward." I ran through all the exercises without any response from him at all.

I couldn't understand it. Now I knew he could do it, that he understood what I wanted. And he'd had *fun*. We had praised him, all of us, making it clear how proud we were of what he'd done. Why wouldn't he do it again?

Back to being Wonderful Mother. It was harder this time— as if Helen Keller had finally understood language but decided not to bother with it after all. Several days passed without a single success, and I got desperate again. "Look, like this . . . put the clothespin on the basket." Sean knocked the basket off the edge of the table. I burst into tears, sobbing. Lost in my own misery, I covered my face with my hands. It's hopeless, I thought. When I looked up Sean was standing in the middle of the room watching me. We stared at each other in silence. On his face was a look I had never seen there before—surprise, I think, and curiosity. He came closer and put one hand on my knee. "Mom?"

I wrapped my arms around him and he touched my cheek, looking at the tears on his fingers. "Cry?" he said, his face sad, open. His arm was around my shoulder and, briefly, he hugged me back. I held him for another moment, then he broke away and began turning the light switch on and off, his face blank. There's a real child in there, I thought. He's trapped and we've got to get him out.

Another week went by. Finally, another success. Sean drew a complete house on the acetate sheet. The idea, of course, was to teach him to see the whole rather than the separate parts of a picture. A simple drawing of a house, for instance, he saw as three unrelated pieces:

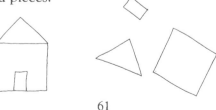

After the house, he traced a snowman, the three parts touching rather than floating in space independently. A few days later he put a row of colored clothespins onto the basket. He was hugged, praised. Yet the next day there would be nothing but refusal; often he swept everything off the table onto the floor. How was it possible that his success didn't lead to other successes? Why didn't he get it? It was as if he had to counter any progress by going backwards.

I had always thought that there was nothing worse than seeing one's child in pain. But Sean's compulsions, his strange behaviors, so clearly comforted him and made him feel safe. The irony was that I was working to force him out of whatever haven he worked so hard to create and, in so doing, I was causing his pain, making him suffer. He wanted to deny human contact. After all, the condition of the world was evidence enough that the most dangerous creature was the human—did Sean simply sense that somehow? Was he on a higher plane, where he recognized that involvement with human relationships was the road to betrayal and loss? Maybe so, I thought, but the truth is that we're all we have, and to permit my son to remove himself from the peril and the joys of human life was to allow him to die.

My mother kept making me do those exercises every day. I was determined not to do what she told me because I didn't want to give her any more reasons to yell at me or disapprove of me. I had no idea that I could fail at something and that she would understand and not yell.

Sometimes I did do what she asked. If I did it right and I knew I wouldn't fail, it got to be a little fun. But the thing was, I never made *any connection from one day to the next. If I did the exercise right on Tuesday, it never connected to Wednesday. Nothing I did ever reinforced what I was supposed to do—I don't know why even now. I had no more ability to make connections than to recognize consequences. Yesterday's success meant nothing to me. The things my mother used for the exercises appeared to be brand-new even if I had just used them correctly the day before.*

Sean, at five years old, had at last begun to say more than the isolated words he had uttered for the past several months. He copied Megan, saying whatever she said, but he was very hard to understand. He seemed to say the words for their sound rather than their meaning, but if he wasn't understood at once, he became enraged. Also, if he managed to ask for what he wanted, he expected to get it immediately—he was tyrannical in his demands.

Most often he said what he didn't want. "No, no, no, no, no!" he'd yell. He seemed to be expressing his anger rather than expecting a result. He said "no" to his toys if they didn't fall the way he wanted, to his clothes if his arm got stuck in the sleeve as I was putting on his shirt.

I knew that Megan could talk and I couldn't, but it didn't really bother me very much. When I did start talking, though, I believed it was a little miracle—it was something I did on my own, after all, and a major accomplishment for me. Other people should see it the same way, I thought, but sometimes they didn't know what I meant when I spoke, and that made me furious! That meant they didn't see the miracle. That was the message I got: They didn't think my accomplishment was important. When Mom and Dad didn't under-stand me, I let them know how angry I was, but if it was my grandmother or grandfather, I hid my feelings.

I thought that if I got angry with my grandparents for not under-standing me, they would turn against me too. My parents hated me, I knew that—why else would they yell at me so often? I couldn't risk making my grandmother hate me or she would never let me come to her house again. My only escape from hell would be taken away from me.

Later in my life, beginning when I was about eight years old, I developed deep feelings of love for my grandmother. At this time, however, she was just the only person who would put up with me, who tolerated my behavior. She was my way of getting away from my mother.

Sean and I made the monthly trips to see Dr. Rossi in Akron alone in our Volkswagen beetle. The car's heater didn't work, so during the winter I had to scrape ice off the inside of the windshield, the flakes forming a pile in my lap as I tried to drive and, at the same time, keep Sean from throwing himself wildly around inside the car.

Dr. Rossi worked with Sean, checking on his progress with the retraining program. At the end of each session he talked to me.

"I need advice, some other way of handling him—I'm out of ideas. Even though he does a few of the exercises now and then, most of the time he refuses. Why?"

Rossi shook his head sadly.

"And everything else is the same or worse. There has to be something else I can do!"

He shrugged and shook his head. "Just keep doing what you're doing—you can see he's made some progress."

But I wanted more. I wanted to know how this had happened to our son. "Look—I had a perfectly healthy pregnancy; I wasn't sick at all. There was just this one thing that I'd even forgotten about . . ."

I told him about an incident when I was three months pregnant. One of Ron's students had invited us to dinner at her parents' home. When we arrived we met her little brother, a three-year-old. The little boy had climbed into my lap; he seemed groggy and listless. "He's sick," his mother explained when she'd put him to bed. "He's got the measles." The measles? This woman knew I was pregnant and she let her child climb all over me? I asked my doctor about it the next day. "Better take a shot for German measles," he said, "just to be on the safe side." I did, and the shot made me sick for several days, with a fever and a vaguely upset stomach. My doctor assured me that the shot would have no ill effect on the fetus.

"Could that have been the cause?" I asked Rossi.

Again he shrugged. "It doesn't really matter, does it?" he said. "Whatever it was or wasn't, you have to find a way of dealing with it *now*. Putting a name to it makes no difference."

"*Yes it does!*" I wanted to shout, as I watched him in silence. I wanted him to tell me that my child had been damaged by a vaccine, that I was blameless in all this.

I had a child I was embarrassed to take places, a child who looked perfectly normal but who behaved in a way I'd never seen before, doing things that humiliated me and made me feel like a total failure as a mother. There was the same question in everyone's eyes—family, friends, strangers—that silently asked, "*Why do you allow your child to act like this?*"

Sean hated going to see Rossi. Once, I took him to an ice cream shop before our appointment, to make the trip less painful for both of us. For some months he had had a phobia about having glasses of water set on the table whenever we ate out; we had to remember to ask the waiter or waitress that none be brought or we faced an inevitable temper tantrum so uncontrollable that we would have to leave the restaurant.

On this particular day I was preoccupied. The car had given me problems on the drive from Youngstown—the engine seemed to be "missing," and I was consumed with the thought that it would cost a fortune to have it fixed and with the fear that we might not make it home. Sean and I were seated at a table beside a huge plate-glass window. I was staring out at the leaden skies of the Ohio winter when Sean screamed.

A waitress was setting two glasses of water on our table. Sean leaped to his feet, upsetting the water and sending his chair flying backwards; it crashed into the window and thudded to the floor. He threw himself down next to the chair, writhing and yelling, his hands clasped tightly over his ears. The window, miraculously, had not broken. The waitress looked from Sean to me. "My God!" she said. I grabbed Sean, yanked him to his feet, and shook him.

I was still shaking when we reached Rossi's office ten minutes later. "Why does he do it? What does it *mean?*" I demanded, after I'd described the incident. "What makes him scream about glasses of water? I can't control him, a five-year-old child, but he controls everything I do—we can't eat in a restaurant, I can't shop in a store, or sit down for ten seconds to think a thought of my own—we have to try and outguess what he's going to do to avoid a scene. What am I going to do?"

Rossi looked at me in silence for a moment, then turned to Sean. "Well, Sean, why did you do that?"

I stared at Rossi. He was waiting for an answer! My God, I thought—a new concept. Ask him! My son had never given an explanation for anything in his life; from all we'd seen, he had no idea that there *was* such a thing as an explanation, as cause and effect. But here I was, watching a clinical psychologist ask an autistic child whose behavior was compulsive, irrational, and bizarre why he acted as he did. I couldn't wait for the answer! Sean twisted away and ignored us both. Rossi stood up and took him into his inner office for the session.

I had a rule about glasses of water when we went out to eat. To me water was tasteless, bland, not exciting. Therefore, it should not be served with a meal in a restaurant. That was my rule. They had to serve something I liked—Coke, for instance. When they brought water and set it down, I got absolutely infuriated! It violated my rule and made me feel out of control and helpless. I knew the waitress or waiter was doing it on purpose to hurt me and make me helpless. I had to show them that my rule was not to be broken!

As I waited, I glanced through the pile of reading material in the room. There were a few truly ancient "women's" magazines but nothing resembling a professional periodical, not so much as a pamphlet on children's problems, on autism. I had already been to the library to read everything I could find on the subject. "Everything" turned out to be one book, *Child in the Glass Ball*, a mother's account of her autistic son. The little boy's behavior was amazingly like Sean's—the same spinning and twisting, the same compulsiveness, the inability to respond. But this little boy was even more remote, enclosed, and was eventually institutionalized. The book scared me to death.

The only other information I'd come across consisted of a few brief accounts in psychiatric and medical journals. Most of the experts referred to autism as childhood schizophrenia; no one knew what caused it and there was no known treatment. I had also read an article about Dr. Leo Kanner, who had coined the word *autism* in 1943; he described it as a psychosis, the symptoms of which were, "the children's inability from the beginning of life to relate themselves to people and situations in an ordinary way and the anxiously obsessive desire for the preservation of sameness"; behavior was marked by the repetition of apparently meaningless acts. Kanner believed that autism was caused by "refrigerator parents," a term that did indeed strike a dagger of ice into my heart. These parents, he said, were highly educated and intelligent but emotionally cold; when the child did not receive warmth and love from the mother at the breast, he retreated, shutting himself off from the outside world. The article enraged me and then left me feeling hopeless and condemned.

When the door opened and it was time for me to see Rossi, Sean looked upset and angry; he was kneeling on the floor as far from the doctor as he could get.

"Well," said Rossi, "I still don't know why he did that with the water glasses; he won't say. But I spanked him."

I couldn't have heard that right. "You what?"

"He has to learn that he can't go around behaving that way!"

"You *spanked* him?" Rossi looked at me and nodded. "But

68

that's what *I* do! I don't want him spanked—for God's sake, that's why we come here, to find some other way of handling him!"

I picked Sean up off the floor and held him a minute. He was shaking, but he didn't look at me.

I never expected him to hit me. I couldn't believe it! Now I thought, "I must be bad! Not only are Mom and Dad spanking me, but this strange man did it as well!"

I have no idea what I actually did to make him hit me—I was not deliberately doing what he told me not to, after all. I was in my shell. I hardly paid any attention to what went on in his office. The room we were in and the instructions he gave were things I tuned out; I didn't pay any attention to him. All I wanted was to get out of there and get back to doing the things I loved. But now he was punishing me for something. From then on, after he spanked me, I had nothing more to do with him. No matter what he said or did, I refused to take it in.

"I won't take him back there!"

"Okay," Ron said, "fine." Silence.

"But the only thing is, he has been making progress, at least a little, since we started going to Rossi."

"I know he has."

"And there are only four months left before he has to go to kindergarten—I'm afraid he'll never make it if we stop now."

"Me too. Besides," Ron said, "he has to get used to being told what to do by other people if he's going to go to school."

"Should we take him back just until school starts?"

"I don't think we have much of a choice."

We told Sean, repeatedly, that Dr. Rossi had made a mistake spanking him, that he would never do it again, and that we were very angry with him for doing it. "We will only go three more times, I said, "then we'll be all through."

I called Rossi on the phone. "I want to make it clear that you are never to hit him again or punish him in any way."

"Whatever you say," he said quietly. "It's up to you. I got very angry with him. I'm sorry I lost my temper."

We continued making the trips to Akron for several more months, until it was time for Sean to begin kindergarten. Ron and I both felt that even if the psychologist seemed crazy, we should carry out the program since there had been at least some progress.

Whatever the cause—the retraining exercises or maturity— we saw changes in our son during the last few months that we used the program. Sean's left-to-right orientation improved, he began to take some pleasure in drawing, both with and without the acetate sheet, the beanbag game had become a real game for the two of us—the first time he had ever played with me at anything—and he often laughed just because he was having fun. I kept hoping these successes would lead to others, that he would begin responding to praise with behavior that we could respond to favorably, that our approval would start to influence his behavior in general. That wasn't the case, however. Reinforcing his "good" behavior never led to more of the same. But so what? I thought. There had been a little progress for the first time in his life, and that was enough for now.

In the spring of that year we had made another trip to Akron to see Dr. Logan. Since the Ritalin didn't seem to have had much effect on Sean's hyperactivity once he had assimilated it, he had replaced it with another medication called Mellaril. That too, though, calmed Sean for only a week or so. Logan had said to continue giving it to him, that often the effects were accumulative. We hated giving Sean medication of any kind and couldn't understand why he should have to take something that didn't help him. Finally Logan agreed that there might be another suitable drug, but before prescribing it he wanted to see Sean again.

The doctor watched Sean for several minutes, asked him questions, had him draw. Sean paid little attention to Logan and refused to follow his instructions. Logan sent him out to the waiting room, then turned to us. "Tell me what he's like now."

I explained that we could still do nothing to modify his behavior, that he was lost in his own world most of the time but that I had been doing the retraining exercises Dr. Rossi recommended and was a little encouraged by Sean's occasional responses.

Logan watched me in silence for a moment. "You'll wish your son had been born blind, deaf, or retarded," he said, "because autism is the worst. And if there is any progress it usually stops at puberty. You have to face it—you may very well have to institutionalize him."

I was numb. There was a buzzing in my ears. I looked at Ron, whose face was white as he stared at Logan. Then a word sounded in my head. *Never.* We will *never* put our child in an institution and we are *not* going to lose him. We had both had glimpses in Sean's eyes of the tormented little boy trapped inside our child's compulsions, terrified of a world he didn't fit into—and somehow we were going to get that child out.

"We don't believe that," Ron said.

Logan looked at us both with the superiority of his greater knowledge. "Just so you're prepared," he said.

He wanted us to try a new medication, Phenergan, with Sean. "It's actually a stimulant," he explained, "but for these kids it usually acts just the opposite way—it's calming and not as strong as the others. Watch him closely and call me at once if you have any problem with it. You probably won't notice the effects for a couple of days."

We gave Sean the Phenergan on Tuesday. By the next day he seemed even more active than usual. On Thursday afternoon he passed into a new plane of hyperactivity. It was as if he were being pursued by a swarm of bees—he ran, yelling, through the house, waving his arms frantically. He bounced off the door-frames, ran into walls. I tried to hold onto him, but he wrenched away. His strength was formidable.

Ron came home from school. Together, we got Sean into his bedroom and closed the door. He climbed onto his book-shelves, jumped off, climbed onto the dresser, jumped off. Ron ran downstairs to call Dr. Logan while I tried to catch Sean, to contain him before he hurt himself. He wouldn't let me touch him. Thank God, I thought, we can still catch Logan at the office!

Ron came back. Logan, he said, was off on a fishing trip to Canada until Monday. He couldn't be reached because there were no phones. He had left no one to cover for him.

We watched Sean ricochet around the room, yelling. I leaned against the wall, stunned. Ron made a grab for Sean as he flew past and caught him. He held him, trying to comfort him; Sean's arms and legs flailed wildly. "Let's try some water— fill up the tub with warm water. Maybe that will quiet him!"

I rushed out into the hall. Megan stood in her doorway, her eyes wide. "What are you doing to him?"

I picked her up and hugged her. "It's not us, honey, it's the new medicine—it's making him worse."

She started to cry. "It's hurting him! Don't give him any more!"

"Oh we won't! Come help me fill up the bathtub so we can calm him down."

The three of us tried to get Sean into the bathroom, but we couldn't manage his writhing body without hurting him. Ron let him go and he took off, tearing around the house, running so fast we couldn't keep him in focus. He sped from room to room, leaping, climbing, and yelling. There's no way he can keep going like this, I thought.

I felt funny. My heart started to race and I was totally out of control. I felt as if I were being chased—I'd go crazy if I stopped so I had to keep going and going.

At one point I climbed up onto some shelves over the stairs and looked down. The danger didn't mean anything to me. I got a thrill out of being so high, and I almost jumped, but at the last second I didn't. I had a deep feeling of euphoria. There was so much pent-up energy inside me that it was like being on a racetrack; I watched the rooms go flying by, faster and faster. I was the fastest person in the world!

Sean ran without stopping until just after three in the morning, when suddenly he sank onto the couch and fell sound asleep. Ron picked him up and carried him to his bedroom. We stood beside the bed and watched him. He seemed to be breathing normally. We looked at each other and tiptoed from the room. We felt ten years older.

That was the end of any medication. It was also the end of Dr. Logan for us. I called him on Monday to tell him about the nightmare the three of us had gone through while he had been fishing in another country.

"Don't give him any more of that medicine," he said. "It's not working for him."

That summer my parents bought us a membership in a nearby swim club, a gift that saved my sanity over the long summer months. Sean liked the water and it visibly relaxed him, but it had not always been that way.

Two years earlier we had used a friend's pool. One-year-old Megan had gleefully flung herself off the diving board into Ron's arms, swimming underwater like a tadpole.

Sean, though, was terrified. At first he refused even to touch the surface of the water with his hands. Ron picked him up and sat on the edge with him on his lap, their feet dangling over the side. Slowly he carried him into the pool, holding him tightly. Sean screamed piercingly and fought to get away, his eyes wide with horror. Ron took him out. Sean crept closer to the edge as if he wanted to try again, so Ron carried him back into the pool. More screaming. Ron kept at it, carrying him in and out, reassuring him that it was safe. At last Sean allowed himself to be carried into the pool, but he struggled to get his hands onto the side, clutching it with all his strength.

The next time we used the pool his fear was the same; he reacted to the water as if afraid it would swallow him. Ron began again, explaining, soothing. He showed Sean how deep the water was on his own body, that the depth didn't change.

In the swimming pool I felt absolute terror. Even though I could feel the bottom of it one minute, I knew that I could be sucked under the next. I had no sense of permanence. I only knew that the pool could be bottomless and that it could kill me. I had to hold on, that was all there was to it. I needed 100 percent assurance that nothing bad would happen to me. The water itself was soothing, and I liked the physical sensation of it. But the thing was—if I let go, would there be a bottom to the pool anymore?

At last, after countless attempts, the screams stopped. Sean held onto Ron and allowed himself to be carried into the pool and away from the side. His head swiveled from right to left as he checked to make sure that nothing was changing, that the water stayed where it was supposed to be.

Many weeks later, he went in alone. He slid into the shallow end of the pool and stood with both hands on the side. It was a triumph. Once he had conquered his terror, he didn't want to get out. For the rest of the summer, every time we used the pool he stayed in the shallow end, bobbing up and down, holding on to the edge. He eventually let go with one hand but never with both—one always remained to anchor him in the unknown.

Now, two years later, he was no longer frightened of the water, but he had developed an aversion to the patches of wet cement that surrounded it. If water had splashed out of the pool and darkened the surrounding area, he refused to walk on it. He crossed it only if the cement were light-colored and dry, as if the damp sections were holes he might fall into. We stood on the patches ourselves, carried him over them, had him touch them with his hands, explained, but could not lessen his fear until one day, more than a month later, he was suddenly no longer afraid.

I hated the dark cement at the swim club. It looked forbidding, just like dark-skinned people such as Dr. Rossi, and I was afraid of it. I knew I could get swallowed up in it, that it was like quicksand. When I was small, I used to have a lot of visions of something grabbing my feet and pulling me down, sucking me under. So when my mom and dad made me touch the wet cement with my hand, it didn't matter to me—it was feet that were vulnerable—very, very vulnerable.

Since Megan preferred the "big people" pool, Sean went there with her, holding on to the side and bobbing up and down in water well over his head while she swam. In a few weeks he began really going underwater, working his way down the side until his feet touched bottom, then shooting to the surface to announce at the top of his voice, *"Five-one!"* The water depths were painted on the sides and he moved from one number to the next. He would momentarily disappear underwater, only to reemerge and shout, *"Five-three!"* Even when he gave up his hold on the side and learned to swim underwater (but not on top of it), he spent all his time investigating the water depth.

I vividly remember a tiny hole on the floor of one of our rooms. It was a knothole in one of the old floorboards, and I loved to squat down and look into it; sometimes I twirled my finger around its edge in much the same way that our washing machine would spin. I would put my finger in as far as it would go to test how deep the hole was and peer into the opening to see how far it went. I knew in my mind that it went to the cellar below me, but I wanted to see what it looked like down there. Mom would say, "Sean, you know that hole goes to the basement," with the hope of quelling my interest, but that was not what I wanted. I had to see for myself, over and over. I needed to test the depth between the hole and the basement floor, although I was fully aware that I would not actually be able to touch the floor, because it was too far away. I used my finger as a point of reference. I had to keep seeing for myself that the hole was at least as deep as my finger was long.

The same thing went on inside me at the pool. I had to keep testing its depth. Knowing that the deepest part was twelve feet did nothing for me. I had to find out for myself by feeling the ledge go down with my foot. I didn't trust the water.

I was worried about Megan, about her being constantly with Sean and isolated from other children. He had begun to tease her incessantly, repeating a word—any word—over and over into her ear until she'd start to scream. Often she hit him to make him go away, but that only made him giggle. He didn't hit back, but he stayed bent over her, whispering his word, until she got up and ran away from him.

Much of the time he ignored her, focused on his world, but she was often drawn into his activities. I was horrified when I saw her rolling toys down the stairs, copying what he did. I knew my fear was irrational, that she grew quickly bored with his repetitions, but I hated the sight of the resemblance, however brief.

Several times we had invited other little girls to the house, but Megan seemed unsure of what to do with them. Clearly they were boring to her, accustomed as she was to her brother's colorful behavior. The most recent little girl had brought along a collection of dolls to play with.

Megan, who at age three spoke like a miniature adult, whispered to me, "Oh no, do you see what she's got?"

"That's okay—try playing with her dolls for a while, then you can both do something you like."

"But I *hate* dolls!"

"I know. So take her up to your room and maybe she'll see something else she's interested in."

Half an hour later Megan was back with a report. "Nope. All she wants to do is play with those dolls."

"Oh."

"Do you think she would mind if I went outside to play?"

"Yes," I said. "I think she would mind."

Megan sighed deeply, then turned and slowly climbed the stairs to her playmate.

The visit ended in chaos. Though I tried to keep Sean away from the little girls, he knew where he wanted to be. He swooped into the room, kidnapped one of the dolls and began chasing Megan with it through the house yelling, *"Here! here! here!"* I grabbed the doll and returned it to its owner, but Sean was back, twirling through the room, knocking over toys, scribbling across Megan's papers. I picked him up and carried him, kicking, out of the room. I smiled down at the little girl. "We'll let the two of you play!" She stared at me. She was only three, but she knew we were all crazy.

So now I had big hopes for the swim club. I was sure there would be other children for Megan to befriend, little girls who were as active as she was. When she did begin playing with another child, though, Sean was always there, calling her name, tugging at her arm. I tried to distract him. He had learned to jump into the pool from the side; I encouraged him to show me how good he was at it, but after a few minutes he was back with his sister. He wanted her attention and he got it. On the other hand, the pool was the one place where he didn't tease Megan, where they actually played together in the water. Keeping him away from her was just another punishment for him, and I couldn't do it. I warmed to the sound of his laughter, watched him really having fun doing what he called "tricks" in the water. Sean's behavior at the pool was the most "normal" I'd ever seen.

We'll wait for fall, I thought, when Megan can go to nursery school. She'll meet other kids there and she'll be fine. For now, Sean needs her—there's no way I can separate them.

During the summer Sean began to really talk. He spoke mechanically, however, without inflection, confusing word order and mixing pronouns indiscriminately. "Her *bad* girl!!" as he pointed at Megan. "Them need to spank she soon!" The word choice might have been wrong, but the meaning couldn't have been clearer.

He called himself "Sean," never "I," and referred to himself in the third person: "He want water right now!" (He continued to refer to himself in this impersonal way for more than two years.)

As I listened to him struggle to master language, I was filled with awe for the way children learn the incredible complexities of speech, easily and instinctively. Like everything else that came naturally to most kids, language was a snarled mass that

Sean had to untangle and make into a pattern that made sense. It was as if he were inventing language for himself rather than learning to reproduce what he had been hearing for years. Maybe, I mused, he had never really heard any of it until now, when he had an obvious need to make himself understood.

The spectre of kindergarten haunted me. September could not be held at bay forever. Except for his sister, Sean had almost no experience with other children. He had never shown the slightest interest in any of the kids in our neighborhood; when they approached him he ignored them completely. There was a set of twin boys who now lived nearby. They made overtures to him but he didn't respond. Once I'd seen them pull Sean's arm through the wire fencing in our backyard until they cut him. They pulled his hair and threw things at him until I ran out and stopped them. Sean reacted to none of it; he appeared unaware that they were there, that they had hurt him. I talked to him anyway, told him that they only wanted him to play with them. He turned away with a blank face.

The summer ended, as I'd been afraid it would. Four months before his sixth birthday, Sean was going to kindergarten. We had told him what it would be like, what he'd do there. I showed him books about school, talked about the teacher (whom I knew), and told him how much he'd like her—he did, as it turned out. She looked surprisingly like my mother and even acted like her—a gentle, soft-spoken woman with enormous patience. Before the school year began we took Sean to meet her and visit her classroom.

When the day arrived, Megan and I took Sean to school. I went inside with him and handed him over to Mrs. Kreidler. He went without a backward glance at me. I stood outside the door for a long time, waiting for his yell. Then I went out to the car and waited with Meg. What's going on in there? I wondered. What could he be doing? Well, I reasoned, she's got my phone number, so we might as well go home. As we drove home Megan asked, "What do you think he's doing in that school? Do you think they'll be nice to him?"

"I hope they will," I said, finding it hard to picture.

The house was silent; it echoed. It felt weird with just Megan and me in it—no one was thundering through the rooms, no one was yelling. And the phone wasn't ringing, as I had expected it would be the second we walked in. I kept picturing that classroom full of kids I had just seen, with Sean in it. I couldn't even imagine how he would behave in a group or how on earth he would perceive his surroundings.

Megan and I played together until it was time to pick Sean up. He came out of the room with some papers clutched in his hand. He said nothing. We talked to him, hugged him, asked him questions, wanted to see his papers. He handed them over as though they had nothing to do with him, answered our questions with "yes" or "no." I had no idea how he felt about any of it. But he'd done it—he'd made it through the first day. Three long hours on his own.

School was very soothing to me in a way. I immediately saw the structure of it, and that helped me feel I had some control. Since I could already tell time when I got there, I knew exactly what would happen when—and that had a calming effect on me. The day was broken up into small parts and I knew exactly what to expect—I could respond to that. When I was in school I could come out of myself a little bit; I could see how other people acted with one another and what they did in a group.

I had known I was different from other kids for a while because I watched others in the neighborhood. Now, in school, I tried very hard to be "normal" and act like them so that I didn't stand out. I did not want to be different because I knew that different was wrong.

So Sean became a kindergartner. He walked into the classroom like every other little kid. Ron and I were dumbfounded. How was it possible?

Before school began, when we had talked to his teacher

about some of his problems, we had not used the word *autism*. After the first week I spoke with her again and did bring it up.

"He's pretty much in his own world," she said. "He doesn't take part in things and he certainly can't sit still, but he'll come along. He'll be all right, I think." Relief flooded through me.

In the town where we lived there was no alternative to public school for Sean. We had investigated our choices and found there weren't any. The special-education classes inside the public schools were the only help offered to children with "problems." This was, after all, at a time before the educational establishment recognized a group called "children with learning disabilities" and provided them with special teachers or tutors separate from the regular classes. The only schools for kids with special problems were private, far away, and so expensive that they were out of reach. We hoped against all odds to keep our son in public school.

Sean's behavior at home, however, grew worse. I was horrified. When he came home from school he hit the front door, shot through it, and tore around the house in a frenzy of activity. It was like an explosion. He turned the lights off and on, rolled toys down the stairs, spun anything that was spinnable. He was deaf to my voice, frantic to get away when I tried to restrain him, enraged with punishment of any kind. I tried to keep him outside after school, but he insisted on going into the house, screaming if I refused him.

My attempts to engage him in any sort of game or quiet activity were useless. He wanted no part of having a story read to him; if he held a book it was to riffle through it as fast as possible, fanning through the pages without looking at them. He did the same thing with playing cards, flipping through them with his thumb. In fact, these were his least offensive habits, and I often allowed him to continue uninterrupted for half an hour or so, though I was well aware of the self-hypnotic effect of these activities—the glazed eyes and the unnerving giggle.

Ron, the most good-natured and kindest man I've ever known, tried his best to be patient with Sean, to mediate between him and me, to be as accepting as possible of the behavior we faced every day. Most of the time he was successful, often diverting Sean at the last moment before my anger boiled over. Occasionally, though, his patience snapped, with dramatic results.

Sean had a metal top that he loved to spin, a toy that had been mine when I was a little girl. With repeated use the rubber guard on the bottom had disintegrated, leaving a sharp metal point exposed. When Sean frantically pumped the top to rotate it as fast as possible, the point made tiny holes in the kitchen floor. Ron told him that he had to take it outside onto the cement sidewalk, that the floor was being ruined. He showed him the holes. Sean ignored him. Frantic spinning, more holes. Ron took away the top and Sean screamed, holding his hands over his own ears as he did. Holding Sean and forcing his son to look at him, Ron said firmly, "Now look—you take this *outside* and play with it. Do *not* use it in the kitchen."

He went back to reading his book; Sean went back to the kitchen. We heard the "thunk, thunk, thunk" begin immediately on the vinyl floor. Ron jumped up and ran into the kitchen. He grabbed the top and stamped on it with his foot, hard. Then he started jumping up and down ferociously until the top was flat as a can lid. Sean watched him. After a moment of shocked horror, I began laughing. Ron joined in and the two of us held on to each other, doubled over in hysterics. Sean looked from Ron to me, his face expressionless—just more baffling parental behavior.

Suddenly, at age six, Sean became addicted to speedometers. When we were in the car he hung over the back seat to watch the "needle" rise and fall. He didn't care where we were going or what we passed—his eyes were on the gauge. When he realized that other cars also had speedometers, his fascination became dangerous. Walking along our street he'd pull away from me and run up to a parked car, peering in the window at the speedometer.

Late one afternoon Sean and I walked along the sidewalk. Megan, on her tricycle, rode ahead of us. Suddenly, Sean darted out into the street. There was a shrill screech of brakes as the driver skidded to a stop. Sean grabbed the outside rearview mirror and pulled himself up onto the side of the car in order to look inside at the needle. The driver was ashen. I apologized as I removed him from her car. She looked at me and shook her head, obviously shocked at my negligence.

Weak and shaking, I took Sean home and put him into his room. "You must never, never do that again—you could have been killed!" He paid no attention. I yelled and shook him. "Sean, *you listen to me!*" There was no expression on his face.

I couldn't allow him outside for even a minute without watching him. And even when I *was* there, holding his hand, he could be gone in a flash.

Several days later I was in the kitchen, the children in the living room. I froze when I heard the sickening squeal of brakes. "Mom!" Megan called. I ran to the front door, which was standing open. A middle-aged man in a suit and wool tweed cap was coming up the front walk, holding Sean by the arm.

"Is he yours?"

"Yes," I said.

"He almost got himself killed—ran right in front of me!" The stranger's face was white with fury and fear.

I muttered apologies and took Sean inside. He had unlocked the screen door, something he had not done before, and gone outside without my knowing. I began to spank him. I was so filled with rage and terror that I couldn't control myself. And even while I was doing it, I knew that spanking didn't help, that it was no deterrent. The pain I was inflicting had no connection in Sean's mind with what he had just done. He felt no remorse, only his own fury that I was interfering with him, and I was having no effect on his future behavior. When he wanted to repeat his behavior the next time, he would. That was all there was to it.

I really loved to look into car windows at the speedometer; my real interest was the red needle. I tried to see as much of the needle as I could—this gave me a strong feeling of joy. I especially liked looking down at the speedometer, because that way I could see more of the needle.

My fascination with speedometers stemmed from a painting we had at home when I was little. I really don't remember too much about the picture itself, but what fascinated me was that the man in it was nude. His genitals were clearly visible—it made me feel quite excited but also confused. I kept thinking, "Will I look like this man someday?" Many times I just went into the room and stared at the painting.

In time my fascination transferred itself to speedometer needles.
The more they were exposed, the more "naked" they looked to me. I
was most thrilled when Mrs. Parker's car was parked on our street
because the needle on her car wasn't tucked away behind the num-
bers panel of the speedometer the way most of them were, and I
could see the tiny round section where the needle actually began.

One day I went out into the road. In the back of my mind I sensed
that a car was coming, but it didn't mean danger to me. My
obsession was too strong and I felt invincible. I had to see the
speedometer! *The man driving the car stopped, grabbed hold of me,*
and took me to the house. I couldn't imagine what I had done—why
was he so angry with me when all I wanted was to look inside his
car? He scared me.

Then Mom got furious with me, and once again I knew that just
because I liked looking at speedometers, I was going to be punished.
It was clear to me that whatever I loved doing was wrong—
especially in this case, when a perfect stranger got angry with me as
well. I couldn't figure out why looking in somebody's car was so
terrible.

After Mom spanked me she gave me a lecture about going into the
street and getting hit by a car. Until then I had not known I could get
hurt in the street. For just one second I was aware of the danger,
while she talked about it, but then it went right out of my head again.
I remember her saying those things, but at the time it didn't connect
to anything I had done or would do.

At this age I lacked an imagination; I simply could not picture
things in my mind. It was many years before I could do so. I wasn't
afraid of moving cars because I couldn't imagine that they could hit
me—to me, a moving car was the same as a parked car, just an
object without potential.

*   *   *

After the speedometer phase, Sean developed a new obsession: dead-end streets. He became frantic if we drove past one without turning in to see where it led. At first we had tried to placate him, driving to the end of the street to satisfy his curiosity if we had time, but that only made his fixation worse. The next time we passed that same street he insisted we turn into it. He knew where it went, we said. It made no difference.

He recognized the dead-end street signs and each time he saw one he wanted us to explore the street. We told him over and over that we could not do what he asked, that we were going somewhere, that we had no time, and so on. He paid no attention, growing increasingly agitated, crying and yelling as we drove on, the sounds bouncing around the car and falling like hammer blows on my brain.

Riding in the car became hell. It had always been somewhat easier to be with Sean when we drove, because not only did the movement seem to soothe him but the car had provided us and him with an escape from the charged behavior that went on inside the house. But it was an escape no more.

I had an intense interest in dead-end streets. The things I liked to do, in general, were those that offered some variation but were still repetitious. So dead-end streets were perfect. I knew the different ways that such streets could look—two neighboring streets could both be dead-ends but look and feel totally unlike each other. Yet they both ended, and in that way they were the same.

So dead-end streets fit my rule—a little variation with a lot of repetition. I loved being in the car and seeing a dead-end sign; I would look up that street for as long as I could, trying to see all the way to the end. Sometimes I could actually see where the street "died," but most of the time I could not. When I couldn't, I desperately wanted to travel up it—that was the only way my curiosity could be satisfied. Questions raced through my mind: Does that street go into the woods before it ends? Does it end in a circle? Does it turn into a driveway and stop? These questions would get into my head and stay there, going around and around.

Most streets just kept going on forever, but I loved the dead-ends because they made me feel safe. Every time we approached one my anticipation would skyrocket. Then what happened? Our car would pass right by! My parents would refuse to turn into the street. I hated that and I got so angry and resentful! It infuriated me when all I wanted was to see the end of a street and they wouldn't let me. All I asked was that they take me up the street, and they wouldn't even do it! I felt deprived of something I really loved; besides, I had to rely once again on someone else to take me, someone else in control. At least if I wanted to throw my play phone into a tree, I could toss it up there on my own! The car was not in my control, so once again Sean Barron could not get what he wanted! I felt tremendous inadequacy and that made me very, very angry.

This was the message I got: They won't take me up this street because they think that something I love is somehow wrong. It didn't take me long to feel that there really was something wrong with me. After all, what harm could it do to drive up a dead-end street? Since I wasn't trying to hurt anybody, why the hell did I have to be hurt? So I formed the perception that I was a bad person and that I had no power. We might pass five dead-ends in a row, and I wouldn't get to go down one of them! Then the next one would be a through street, and inevitably that would be the one my parents chose. I got furious!

So the next time we drove past those same streets I would turn my head to look down each dead-end, but when we came to the through street I would only look straight ahead or in the opposite direction, *pretending that the street* did not exist! *In this way I showed that I had power over the street as well as over the people in the car. I'd think, "They can make me go down this street, but they can't make me see it or accept it as real."*

In addition to his mania for dead-end streets, Sean developed what appeared to be a terror of left turns. When Ron or I switched on the left-turn signal he'd begin to scream, "No! Don't do that! No, you *can't!*" His screams were deafening. Why this? Where the hell did he get what seemed an actual fear of left turns? *Left turns??*

He started refusing to go in the car with us if he thought we might be turning left at some time on the projected trip—a good possibility indeed. So we had a fight on our hands even before we could get out the door. Usually it ended with one of us carrying him, kicking and fighting, to the car and stuffing him into it. Just another jolly family outing.

We explained to him every way we could think of what we were doing and why, that not liking left turns made no sense, was stupid. We got no response. The obsession grew worse and continued until Sean was over seven, when it was replaced by a new set of rules of his own devising.

I hated it when I was in the car and we had to make a left turn. I had no particular feelings about right and left per se—it only mattered when we were in the car. As soon as they put on the left turn signal I got infuriated. It was simple—a left turn was "dumb" and a right turn was "better." Now I no longer know why I felt that way, but at the time it was just true—it was a conviction I had.

I equated a left turn with stupidity—and since my parents thought I was dumb, every time they made a left turn they were making a statement against me. They were saying I was stupid. I felt no anger if we turned right. When we did turn left, I leaned in that direction, counteracting the natural pull of the car—that way I made it seem as if we were really turning right instead.

When I got into the car I had to sit on the right side of the back seat and Meg had to sit on the left because the right was better. *Sometimes, to deny we were turning left, I slumped way down in the back seat so I couldn't see which way the car was going.*

So now I was compelled to map out in my head where we were about to go in the car. I figured out the route, turn by turn, so that I could count the number of right and left turns we would have to make. If there were too many left turns, I refused to go along. When my parents made me go anyway, I was furious with them. I was mad not only because I wasn't given a choice but also because something I disliked was going to happen not once, but many, many times. Those car trips were very hard on me, and I got angry even before we had to get into the car. I dreaded all those left turns, and I got yelled at for refusing to go but was forced to go anyway!

We bought a new house. It was two miles away in another small town called Boardman. It had become impossible to have both kids on the second floor with our bedroom on the first. They were too isolated that way; we couldn't protect Megan from Sean's invasions as he ran wild through her room, taking whatever he wanted.

The "new" house was old and needed a lot of work. Ron did all the carpentry on weekends; I painted all the walls and woodwork, working at night when Ron was at his second job, directing at the TV station. Both children slept at my parents' house while I thrived on the hard, physical labor—a release for the anger, tension, and frustration of my days. Removing wall-paper, scraping cracked paint, sanding the old wood until my arms ached—it was like a vacation. I loved it all, not least because I was alone.

We were both apprehensive about the actual move. What would Sean make of it when he hated even the smallest change? To make things even worse, it was the middle of the school year, and he would be transferred to a different kindergarten class.

We would have much more space than in the old house. Our new bedroom separated Sean's from Megan's, so she had a better chance of privacy. The school was just a short walk away, and it was the same school system in which Ron was a teacher. The only disadvantage was that the yard was huge and unfenced, making it harder to watch Sean, easier for him to disappear.

———————

They told me we were going to move. I didn't much like the idea at first. They drove me past the new house. I could see that it was bigger than the other one. There was something that appealed to me—there was a mystery to the new house. I always liked mystery: Where did the rooms lead? Were there clothes chutes? What was inside the closet doors? Were there holes in the floors? Actually, as it turned out, that good feeling overpowered my not liking change—for some reason it didn't make much difference to me that we were moving to a new house. Besides, I knew that there would still be things I liked: light switches, registers, our washing machine. By the time they were ready to move, I had already gone through the new house and knew exactly where all the light switches were in all the rooms.

Sean was drawn to the washing machine and dryer in the new house. Whenever he could he slipped down the cellar stairs to watch and listen to the clothes spinning. I'd find him there, leaning on the washer, giggling to himself.

One day I washed all our winter jackets and put them into the dryer. When I took them out they were covered with huge blotches of bright color. Sean had thrown a bunch of crayons into the dryer with the clothes, and the heat had melted the wax, affixing it permanently to the jackets. Hundreds of dollars worth of coats were ruined.

When I found him, I took him downstairs and showed him what he'd done. I knew he didn't comprehend cause and effect, but I told him anyhow. "Look. I have to throw out all our jackets," I told him. "*You* did this. You put the crayons in the dryer; they melted from the heat and stuck to the cloth. Now I have to throw them away." I stuffed them into a trash can in front of him. "See?"

He seemed to pay no attention. He looked irritated. But he was in school now—he sat at a desk, like other kids. If I didn't make him listen, would he ever learn that his actions had consequences?

What if he woke up in the middle of the night and my words came back to him, hit some area in his brain that *could* respond? I couldn't accept that he wasn't understanding; what if some day—next Tuesday, next month, in ten years—he suddenly could grasp cause and effect, but I had stopped trying to make him understand? Then he would be hopeless.

I also worried about Sean's diet. Since the beginning of his life he had eaten the same type of food; with age, nothing had changed. I still had no success in getting him to try fruits or vegetables, and his craving for carbohydrates was even greater than before. It wasn't that he'd taste something and decide he didn't like it—the food never reached his lips. He'd touch it with his hands, sniff it, and refuse to have anything further to do with it. He appeared to have an overwhelming physical revulsion to most foods, especially to anything that was a mixture of ingredients. He wouldn't taste stews or that mainstay of Ohio cooking—the casserole. The only soup he ate was chicken noodle and then only the blandest variety, without vegetables or visible spices.

I had a big problem with food. I liked to eat things that were bland and uncomplicated. My favorite foods were cereal—dry, with no milk—bread, pancakes, macaroni and spaghetti, potatoes, and milk. Because these were the foods I ate early in life, I found them comforting and soothing. I didn't want to try anything new.

I was supersensitive to the texture of food, and I had to touch everything with my fingers to see how it felt before I could put it in my mouth. I really hated it when food had things mixed with it, like noodles with vegetables or bread with fillings to make sandwiches. I could never, never put any of it into my mouth. I knew if I did I would get violently sick.

Once when I was very small, I tried to eat a banana for my grandmother, but I couldn't do it. So from then on I refused to eat any of the other fruits. I wanted to eat the things I was used to; the others were very threatening to me. When Mom tried to get me to eat something new I got very angry with her—I knew what I wanted!

There were other things I had to do every day that made me quite uncomfortable as well. One of these was taking a bath. I felt acutely uncomfortable sitting upright in the bathtub, so I didn't enjoy taking a bath in the least. I absolutely hated the way my bottom felt against the tub, and I couldn't make myself think about something else so I wouldn't feel it. When I tried to sit normally it felt "squishy," and I was extremely sensitive to this feeling. I couldn't shake it off. It was the same feeling I used to have when I couldn't stand to touch our rugs with my bare feet. To make it more bearable, I shifted most of my weight onto one side so that only a part of me came into contact with the bathtub. When they insisted I "sit right," it only compounded the problem. I had no choice—I had to sit in an unnatural *way, so baths were a trying experience. Also it made me feel that there was something wrong with me because I had to sit that way.*

Sean completed the year of kindergarten and was promoted to first grade. We were stunned. Then we were overjoyed. We looked at his report card—all those little "Needs Improvement" boxes were checked; the note from his teacher said that he had no measurable concentration span, that his cooperation and direction-following were very poor, his "interaction" with his classmates nonexistent—but what the hell, he was in first grade!

We had looked at every bit of work he had brought home through the year. He was learning to make letters, he could print his name, he had completed many of the reading-readiness papers. The drawings he made went from odd to bizarre (mostly unrecognizable forms, very "immature" for a child of six, the teacher told us), but there they were, on paper, in color, on the refrigerator.

Both kids and I passed the summer at the swimming club. Ron was still working nights at the TV station, but rather than having the summer days free, he drove every morning to Kent State University, fifty miles away, where he was working on his master's degree. So on nice days—and under the circumstances I defined that as a temperature above 32 degrees under any sky not crisscrossed with streaks of lightning—the three of us went to the pool.

The summer was a repeat of the year before, Megan swimming everywhere, Sean working his way down the sides and shooting forth to announce the water depth. I began to see that we were isolated among a group of people. Occasionally a little girl encountered Megan and they played together for a while, but the parents always seemed to have a reason to remove their child from Meg's company. Sean and Megan were together constantly, and it was quite clear that Sean was "odd," that there was something wrong. The swim club members were white, professional men and their wives—many of them women for whom it would have been a disgrace to have a job outside the home. Things were done very much the same way by everyone—the correct clothes were worn, the right Protestant values adhered to. So most of the club members did the only thing they knew how to do when faced with aberrant behavior among them—they ignored Sean and his whole family.

Megan, only four years old, was to go to kindergarten in the fall, entering school a year early as a result of a testing program that placed her above her age group. The psychologist who tested her had said, "Because of her high IQ, I'm going to recommend that she begin school this year, since I'm afraid that by next year she would be bored with the work. However, she is socially immature for her age, so you'll want to watch her closely for any problems." I took his advice.

The thought of our little girl going to school drenched me with feelings of loss and a sadness too deep for tears. I couldn't let her go, it was too soon! I felt that I hadn't spent nearly enough time with her yet—I'd wasted the precious time we'd had together by giving Sean all my attention, negative though it was. Megan had been so easy to care for, to be with—interested, funny, reasonable, responsive. Sean, on the other hand, certainly was not fun to be with, and nothing was ever easy for him. Almost everything he did was "wrong," and much of the time I couldn't stand the sight of him.

I wanted to start over with Megan. This time I wouldn't waste my days trying to correct Sean, trying to change what couldn't be changed (but, I realized, these issues were all about *me*, not her). The psychologist was right—by next year all the kindergarten work would be too easy, and she hated doing anything easy. I couldn't do that to her.

She was a child wondrously happy with her own pursuits. She woke up every morning full of positive energy. She invented her own games, painted, read her books. She loved every living creature she met. She had two parakeets, two frogs, a dog, and Chip, a praying mantis. Since she couldn't bear to give Chip flies, she decided to try offering him dog food on a wire. I explained that it would never work, that Chip had to catch his own food as it flew by him, but she was undaunted. And sure enough, Chip hooked one arm over the wire Megan held and munched contentedly on the bit of dog food. She was ecstatic. He also, it turned out, was a female. One day we discovered a new egg case, and the next spring, long after Chip had died and been ceremoniously buried, the case split and thousands of baby Chips filled our porch.

She had a bedroom filled with pots of bulbs she was growing, and a little garden in the backyard as well. She could play outside for ten straight hours and still not want to come inside.

Despite being a child in an age dominated by television, Megan never watched it. The year before she had lost interest in the only show she had really liked, the Sunday-night Disney program. At the end of one of the animal stories she had always liked so much she said, "The trouble with these is that they're all the same—a family gets a wild animal pet, then it grows up and gets in trouble, and they have to give it to the zoo. All they do is make it about different animals." She never watched the show again.

The end of summer was a time filled with anxiety. After one year of nursery school three times a week, how would Megan adjust to being the youngest in kindergarten? How would I adjust to her being gone? And how would Sean do in first grade—the real thing, with real grades, learning to read and do arithmetic, and, no doubt the most important thing, having to stay in a classroom for a whole day? It was inconceivable.

The morning school opened Sean was uninterested in the whole thing. He was withdrawn, unresponsive, unable (or unwilling) to make any attempt to dress himself, to follow my simplest direction. After a struggle, he was ready.

When I walked them both to school, I was weak with fear. Megan bounced along, talking about how she wanted to learn to read more than anything else in the world—she thought they would teach her by afternoon, then she'd stay home with her books for the rest of her life. Sean said nothing. Megan's attempts to share her excitement were met with silence. He's never going to make it, I thought with dread certainty. He is in a world he inhabits alone; he's nothing at all like the other kids. It's a cruel fantasy to hope he can somehow fit into a system he can't begin to understand. I almost turned around and took him home with me, but at the last moment I let him go. He walked into his new classroom without hesitating, and I took Megan to her kindergarten room.

When I got home I walked through the house, picking things up and putting them back down without looking at them. I'd start to do something, then forget what it was. I was waiting, of course, for the phone, the angry voice that would say, "Come at once and get your son. How could you bring him here and expect any teacher to put up with this child?"

But no one called. I went to meet Megan at noon. She bounded out the door full of enthusiasm, trying to tell me everything at once. We went home and spent the afternoon together. At one point she looked up at me and said, "How do you think he could be doing, Mom?"

We both went to get him at 2:15. On the way home he was silent, not answering our questions. When he reached the house he exploded, tearing through the rooms knocking things over, yelling.

———————

School was enjoyable to me. Of course, the big thing was that the structure was exactly the same every day. One of the things I really liked to do was to test crayon colors—how dark Pine Green really was compared to other dark shades, or how light Spring Green was on a piece of paper. I could compare colors for hours at a time, and school wasn't really that long. I liked paint in the same way—the dark colors mostly resembled black; therefore, both the dark paints and the dark crayons were mysterious to me. Even though Midnight Blue looks black, I'd think, how dark will it really be if I try it on paper? It was so fascinating to explore different colors that looked the same but really weren't the same as black. Often I made rainbows consisting only of my dark colors. I loved to compare the way they looked on paper to the way they looked on the crayon itself. The light colors didn't interest me because I could tell what they would look like on paper. Black, though, was different. It was a color I couldn't "see." I could, of course, see the crayon itself, but not the actual *color. What made black? Was it possible to find a crayon even darker than black? These kinds of questions kept me fascinated for hours, and my fascination carried over to the other dark colors as well.*

To this day, we don't know how Sean managed to stay in school. We did have one undeniable advantage—Ron was a teacher in the same school system where Sean was a student. We knew many of the teachers, as well as the principal and superintendent. It was obvious that they made a real effort to accommodate Sean and us. Years later one of his teachers told us that when she gave an instruction to the class, Sean would begin to bang his head against his desk. He would continue to do so unless she came to him and explained the directions over again, slowly and patiently, until he understood.

Still, had he behaved in class the way he did at home, no teacher could have allowed him to remain. Somehow, the pressure of twenty-five other kids, the teacher's authority, and the regimentation and regularity of the schedule kept him in check. On conference day his teacher told us, "Well Sean tries, but things aren't easy for him. And he should pay more attention." We were thrilled.

It was clear that Sean was not an easy pupil. At the end of his first-grade year he was promoted, and we received a note from his teacher. It began, in lovely script, with an explanation of how difficult Sean had been to handle; then the handwriting began to deteriorate as she described his erratic and often disruptive behavior until, at the end of the note, we could barely decipher the final sentence. As far as we could tell, she wrote that she was leaving the teaching profession and taking early retirement.

Sean's language was unlike that of the other six- and seven-year-olds. He used prepositions indiscriminately and still referred to himself in the third person. I'd say, "Why did you do that?" and he'd reply, "Sean does not know." He never used language to communicate feelings, thoughts, or problems. What he said sounded as if he had learned it by rote. He didn't tell us anything. He did answer questions to a limited extent—by replying as briefly as possible, often inaccurately, usually with only "yes" or "no"—but 90 percent of the time he *asked* questions—oh, how he asked them! His questions had to do with whatever he was fixated on at the moment: What time is it? (even though he knew quite well how to tell time). How deep is this water? How far does this hole go? How big is this? But our answers rarely, if ever, satisfied him. We tried to show him, if possible, but that never worked either; it was as if he wanted something else, something more, but we couldn't make out what it was.

He asked the same questions over and over, thousands of times. He had no regard for where we were or for what we were doing. Sometimes when we'd say, "You know the answer to that," he'd giggle, other times he'd explode in anger. We knew his questions came from anxiety, from some fear. But of what? We had no idea how to give him any relief.

When he was in kindergarten we had bought him a wooden puzzle of the United States, each piece the shape of the state with a composite chunk for New England. He could put the puzzle together instantly, either faceup, upside down, or face-down, showing only the brown backing. He could recite the names of all the states and their capitals. He plagued us with state questions for more than three years: How far is Vermont? How far is Iowa? What is the capital of Maine? He wanted us to answer, and he became enraged if we refused to respond to his steady stream of questions. We usually gave him the first few answers, but inevitably the answers made it worse—his questions increased and became frantic-sounding. It felt as if we were on a merry-go-round that kept going faster and faster until it became a nightmare. He knew every single answer to all his questions—what the hell did he want? I thought maybe it was just the sound, the give and take of a pattern of speaking, that he craved. So I tried nursery rhymes, easy repetitive poems that we could say. He paid no attention.

His questions became a litany when we had guests to the house:

"How many states have you been to?" he'd begin.

"Oh, about twenty, I guess."

"Have you been to Wyoming?"

"No, not that one," the trusting visitor would reply.

"Have you been to Arizona? To Oregon? To Utah?"

The guest would begin to feel uncomfortable as the intensity of the questions increased. I'd try to derail Sean but it was no use. Finally, either Ron or I had to take him away forcibly, crying and furious.

No other conversation was possible while he was in the room. Once a close and patient friend allowed him to go through all fifty states with his "Have you been to . . ." questions, believing that when he had run through all of them he'd be satisfied. At the end, Sean began all over again. There was never an end.

It was apparent that he needed to control conversations. Since he didn't seem to understand what other people said, he tried to force all of us to take part in his own rituals. Always, it was lists, order, repetition.

Certain words and behaviors, always unpredictable, sent him into a frenzy. *"No!!"* he'd scream. *"He can't sit there!"* Or another time, *"No—she used the word 'cold'!"* and he'd throw himself down on the floor or the ground in tears. It embarrassed me acutely—he did it anywhere, with anyone, and I couldn't come up with any reasonable explanation for the shocked by-standers. Usually I pretended it was normal behavior—rather silly, but you know how kids are.

Sometimes it was what people said that set him off, other times it was what they were wearing, how they moved, where they stood. Often he wanted no one in the room to smile, no one to wear the color blue. I didn't know what to make of it or what to do about it.

For as long as I can remember, I have needed to compartmentalize important things. That is why I had an overwhelming desire to ask people which states they had visited or which ones they had never been to. I liked to look at the shape of the United States and to study the contours of each state. I also liked to study where each state was in relation to the others. My favorites were the ones farthest south because, I thought, it never snowed in those states and the weather was better than in Ohio. It was those states that I chose to draw.

I had a driving need to ask questions about the states because I felt I could not talk the way "normal" people talked, nor could I take part in their conversations, since I didn't understand them. Everyone else talked effortlessly, their conversations flowing as smoothly as a creek, and I felt very inferior, shut out, less impor-tant. I had to compensate for what was lacking, and what better way than to show people that I knew all fifty states, their positions on the map, the shapes of each one? I needed to show everybody how smart I really was, and by asking the questions, I was doing just that. I never asked, "What states have you been to?" but rather, "Have you been to Montana?" so that I could show them I knew all the states.

These questions were also a form of escape for me. When I asked about Montana, for example, I would picture myself there instead of where I really was. I may not have had a very accurate picture of Montana in my mind, but I did know that it was far away from Ohio, and, consequently, from me. So in a way I was at least temporarily removing myself from the pain of my present situation.

I hated the state of Ohio. I didn't like its size or its location on the map. My parents bought me a globe because I loved to talk about states so much, but as soon as I got it, I scratched out Ohio with my fingernails and peeled off all the neighboring states as well. I never even looked at the other countries on the globe. Mom got furious with me for ruining my globe, and I couldn't tell her why I had done it.

I never asked a single person if she or he had been to Pennsylvania. The reason was that it bordered Ohio and was very close to us. Once in a while, however, I did ask if someone had been to Michigan, Indiana, West Virginia or Kentucky, all states that also border Ohio, but were farther away from Youngstown, where I was.

Another thing I liked about the states conversation was its structure. I tried to talk to whomever it was for as long as they'd let me, and I never once got tired of the conversation. I would ask about all fifty states if no one stopped me. This made me know I was in control of the conversation. Even if I couldn't talk the way everyone else did, I could dominate and control what was said; after all, I did *have fifty states to choose from. I wanted to get attention for something other than the things I did that were wrong!*

Looking back, I realize I conducted conversations that were fragmented and disjointed, that led nowhere. At the time, however, what mattered was that doing it made me feel a little closer to being a normal human being. I got recognition, and I felt powerful for at least a while when I steered the talk where I wanted it to go.

His list of rules grew. We had to sit in certain chairs. He demanded that certain answers be given in response to his statements, that uncontrollable things occur at specific times— on school days he absolutely *had* to reach our front door at precisely 2:20 every afternoon. We didn't give in to his demands, of course, and our refusal to do so infuriated him.

He had some kind of fixation with school-bus numbers. He knew all the numbers of all the buses that passed our house. He insisted that they be in a particular order. As soon as he got home from school he raced to the front window to watch them go by, saying each number as it appeared. He was highly excited, giggling to himself. If, however, the buses did not pass in the "right" sequence, he fell apart—crying, yelling. He'd shout, "Yes, it *was* bus number 3—it was *not* bus 14!" It was clear that he needed to control the world around him, that his failure to do so tormented him. I'd see his face contort with pain, and I'd reach out for him, to hold him, to soothe him. How could a little boy bear such constant suffering? He'd twist away from me angrily.

He made up a bus game with playing cards, pretending that the cards were the school buses. He assigned the cards numbers and moved them in strict order, tearing them into pieces if they "moved" incorrectly. This obsession with school-bus numbers continued throughout grade school and into middle school.

I loved the sameness of all the buses—they were all the same color and had the same words on them—but there were minute differences too; for instance, the number on each was different, and there were differences also in the shapes of the "noses" (some very pointed, others rather blunted). My goal was to see all the buses the school owned in one year so I could compare all of them. I loved the way they looked when they were all parked in a line, and I got very angry when bus 24 was late and I had to go home before I saw it. It was not supposed to do that! It was supposed to be in that line with the other buses. I hated it because it behaved the worst and was often late.

One day I lined up my marbles at home just like the buses. I picked four colors to represent the four buses that came to my grade school. The blue ones were bus 24. Then I moved the marbles the way the buses were supposed to move—I moved the other three colors away from the blue ones. Next I put the blue ones where they had been—like bus 24 arriving late. I stared at them. I got so angry seeing the blue marbles by themselves like bus 24 that I threw them down the register.

I started playing the same game with cards. When the card representing bus 24 was "late," I ripped it to pieces!

On school mornings there were many times when Sean refused to come into the kitchen for breakfast. Instead, he'd run through the house knocking things over, yelling, playing with the light switches. Then he'd go back upstairs to his room, returning in a few minutes with a bright, and very fake, smile on his face.

"Good morning. I just got up!" he'd declare. I'd smile, tentatively, and look at him. What was this?

It was Megan who came up with the cause for his tantrums. Sean *had* to be the first person to enter the kitchen every morning or the day was ruined. If any of us got there before him, we violated his sense of order and the day "went bad," as he put it. We watched, and she was right. We tried explaining to him that we were not going to get up "in order," that some days one of us had to leave earlier, that he could not make that kind of rule for all of us to follow. He paid no attention. If Megan reached the kitchen first he threw himself down on the floor, wailing, *"No! no! noooo!"*

Then he'd refuse to speak to any of us or to acknowledge that we were even there. He could not be talked out of his black mood, and he often stayed in it until he went to bed that night.

Mom and I would start fighting no more than ten minutes after I woke up—it was like World War III! My rule was that I was to be the first person downstairs every single morning. That way I could see how everyone else sat down—exactly the way I watched the buses park at school. If my rule was broken, I would be in a terrible mood at once. I would remain silent and not say a word to anybody. When I was in a bad mood, I wanted to withdraw.

Then Mom would get angry with me! She'd make everything twenty times worse—how could I smile and be nice to her or to the others when my rule had just been broken by them? She'd shout that I was being unfriendly, and I'd yell at her because, after all, I was certainly mad enough, and then we'd be at it. When I refused to smile or to speak to her in the mornings, it was not because of her, so what right did she have to be pissed with me?

I was getting angrier and angrier; sometimes, to keep from blowing up completely, I'd leave in the middle of it all, go upstairs, then come back and pretend it was the first time I'd seen her that day. It didn't work very well, though—it infuriated me that in spite of my efforts to start the day over again, Mom wouldn't let me.

Whenever we had our fights in the mornings, I left for school extremely embarrassed—so much so that I couldn't look directly at anyone. I believed that none of the other kids had trouble with their families. What would they think of me if they knew how Mom and I fought? Nothing felt worse than getting on the bus in the morning to face thirty other kids when, just moments before, Mom and I had been screaming at each other.

I tormented and teased Mom to get back at her, but our horrible relationship took its toll on me, too. Every time I teased her a disturbing realization came over me—I really could not control what I did.

We continued to ask about help for Sean—wasn't there a psychologist we could take him to?

"Not here in town, no," our guidance-counselor friend said. "I've never found anybody I'd take my own child to."

"You know exactly what will happen," another friend told me. "They're Freudians—they'll tell you it's your fault and make you feel even worse than you do, and they won't help Sean. Believe me, we've been through just that with our son! You've read Bettelheim; you know what the current thinking is: *The mother did it!*"

Just a month or so earlier I had indeed read Bruno Bettelheim's book on infantile autism, *The Empty Fortress*. I finished it in one day. The book focused on breast-feeding—not doing it enough, or right, or smothering the baby with the breast. When Ron got home that night I told him about it, reading aloud some of the passages I had marked. Bettelheim wrote, for example, that "if things go wrong and the baby's anticipatory behavior is not met by an appropriate response in the mother, the relation of the infant to his environment may become deviant from the very beginning of life."[1] But even if she did breast-feed "correctly," she was still not off the hook! Bettelheim claimed that "the mother's unconscious motives are experienced by the child as a threat to his very existence."[2] And my favorite passage: "Throughout this book I state my belief that the precipitating factor in infantile autism is the parent's wish that his child should not exist."[3]

"How dare he say that?" Ron fumed. "He's got his mind made up that it's the mother's fault, and yet he says 'his' child—that old, all-inclusive masculine pronoun! I love the way the assumption is made that the woman's subconscious is the real culprit, and of course no one can defend herself against that charge! Great—it's just the kind of help we need! So what does he recommend doing with these 'awful' mothers?"

"Just taking the child away from them. He says the child must be removed from the home and undergo intensive psychotherapy."

"How could anyone believe what he says?"

But, as we were to discover, almost everyone did.

In his schoolwork Sean showed marked ability in some areas. He was very good at math, as long as it was concrete. He memorized easily, spelled remarkably well, and had a large vocabulary. When he read or saw a word he didn't know, it infuriated him. It was hard for us to determine how much he *did* know, but his schoolwork was always at least average, often higher—except in assignments requiring abstract reasoning. Then he was lost and confused.

Sometimes we'd watch a children's show on television together. After it was over we'd ask him about it: Why did they give the monkey to the zoo? Why was the little boy crying? He never knew. I read to him and asked him questions about the story as we went along. Nothing. He was too restless to be interested for long, and when he watched television, he seemed to look toward the screen but not really at it. We had no idea what he was taking in, how he was interpreting anything.

Always it was details that caught his attention—the thread on a jacket, a bent corner on the page of a book, a flickering light. These were the things he noticed. Why?

———

I was afraid of my first- and second-grade teachers; their assignments, therefore, seemed menacing. I was frightened that they would spank me, though they never did. It would have been the ultimate embarrassment.

I liked the programmed reading we had because it was quite structured and orderly, but when I didn't know something, I got very angry. The stories we read didn't make sense most of the time—I didn't know why things happened in them, and it was extremely frustrating to me. It seemed that everyone else understood but I didn't.

Besides reading I felt pretty comfortable at school, at least inside the classroom. The work we had to do kept me safe, for one thing, and for another, I never really had to make eye contact with the other kids—if I sat in the back, I saw only the backs of their heads; if I sat in the front, they were behind me.

On the playground it was different. There I stayed in my shell unless I had a chance to tease somebody. The playground was dangerous because the other kids were all around me, and they could do whatever they wanted to me. Now I realize that because I felt so negative about myself, I assumed that they would too and that they would try to hurt me. Although no one ever attacked me throughout grade school, I never lost my fear of being on the playground with the other kids, so I tried never to make eye contact with them.

There was no peace. If I wasn't yelling at him, I was speaking through clenched teeth or sending him to his room—a room that was itself a testimonial to the combat conditions we lived with, the walls scarred and cracked, the woodwork pitted, the furniture scratched and chipped, the toys broken.

Ron and I developed our own ritual. Every night, when our son was finally asleep, I became filled with remorse, with suffocating guilt. I'd watch him as he slept, his face sweet and peaceful. Why did I continue to hit him? I knew it didn't stop him. Why had I spent another day screaming at everything he did? Why couldn't I just ignore most of it? What was wrong with me that made me do the same useless things over and over? He didn't respond to my yelling but Megan did, looking frightened and sad as the battle raged around her. Everything Sean heard coming from me was negative, critical. How could I have allowed myself to fall into that destructive pattern yet again? I knew better; he didn't. I could stop; he couldn't.

"Okay, this is it," I'd say to Ron. "From now on I'm going to stop reacting. I've got to look harder for things to praise." We knew what message Sean got: I'm a bad boy and everything I do is wrong. Megan is good. She's the one they talk to, I'm the one they yell at and hit.

Ron would hold me. We'd talk over the day, comforting each other for our failings, our short tempers. I hated the awful things I had said to my child, the way I felt about him most of the time. It couldn't be as bad as it seemed—I had to get it into perspective. After all, I loved Sean. I knew he was a victim of terrible compulsions, helpless in the face of fears I could only guess at. I couldn't keep punishing him for that, for something he couldn't help.

I would become filled with strength and determination. I *was* going to change and make it all different. This nasty, violent person wasn't me, after all—it was completely against my nature to act the way I had been acting.

In the morning I'd wake up clutching my resolve. Sean would appear. He'd throw his shoe down the stairs and I'd smile and ignore it. He'd see Megan come out of her room, sleepy-eyed and grinning at me. *"No!"* he'd scream. "She can't smile like that—stop her!" Her grin would disappear.

"You leave her alone!" I'd yell back. Megan would turn away from the sound of my voice, her gaze darkening. In his presence for less than two minutes, I had lost my resolve, and my good intentions lay in shreds around my feet.

When Megan was in first grade and Sean in second, I decided to go back to school. I wanted to begin teaching as soon as possible, so I was determined to get my degree in less than two years. That meant I had to take an overload of course work, between twenty-two and twenty-four hours each quarter. Since the maximum number of hours allowed by the university was eighteen, I had to overlap a few courses; with a combination of double-talk and forged signatures, I got the hours I needed.

I took classes straight through every day, from 9:00 until 2:00, so that I could leave home after the kids left for school and be back before they got home. I had a lot of work to do at night—the meaningless busywork that education courses always seem to require plus a lot of reading for my literature and science courses.

Ron had received his master's degree earlier in the year, after years of night classes, and now he took over the care of the children in the evenings. When they were asleep he often did my lesson plans for me—rescuing me when I sat on the floor in tears, my mind a blank, faced with having to do an outline for teaching a pretend lesson in, say, "Our Neighbors in Canada" to a group of my classmates pretending to be third-grade social-studies students. I could manage Shakespeare, geology, new math, and the British novel, but the absurdity of the education courses nearly defeated me.

116

I got a teaching job when Sean was nine, Megan seven. I taught reading to sixth graders in a school where the kids changed classes every forty-five minutes, so each teacher had about 140 students a day. I tried to individualize the instruction as much as possible, using books and magazines in place of textbooks, writing plays for the kids to perform and tape record, reading aloud from many of my favorite children's books. It was draining and exhausting, more time-consuming than I'd ever imagined. But at the same time it was rewarding and stimulating. Collectively, the kids were never as hard to handle as my own son. There were no behavior problems comparable to his, no failure that could equal the way I felt I had failed with him. Some of my students might be slow, dull-witted, bored, disruptive, or retarded, one or two were even psychotic—but with nearly every one, if I worked like hell, I could get to them; I got a response and saw a change, some progress. At home, with Sean, I saw no improvement. Some of his behaviors had altered, true, but for the most part they had simply evolved into different, often worse, behaviors.

Sean still didn't "talk" to us. His language stayed "memorized," repetitive, meaningless to us, even a source of anger, because when I believed he had asked a real question, I'd discover I'd been "used," that his question was linked to a chain of words he wanted to hear:

"What does S 128 X mean?"

"I don't know—where did you see that?"

"*Nooo!* You say, 'License plate from New Jersey'!" he'd yell.

Then he became fascinated with murders and murderers, and the scenario would go something like this:

"Where is Ligonier?"

"It's a town in Pennsylvania, not too far from here."

"Where is Harris Avenue in Ligonier?"

"I have no idea—why?"

He'd giggle and not answer. Then it would hit us that there had recently been a sensationalized murder there which, of course, Sean had heard all about—he knew all the answers to his own questions. We tried to discuss the subject with him, attempting to get at his feelings, his fears. "That man is in prison now, Sean—are you afraid of him?"

He didn't understand, or he didn't make the connection, or . . . who knew what. Was he afraid we'd murder him? Or that he'd murder us? Or both? We didn't know.

———

I was fascinated with certain murder cases—with murderers like Lee Harvey Oswald and Charles Manson. Since I was being yelled at all the time, I believed that I was a horrible person—it was a belief so deeply imbedded that I thought I was as bad as those men. Although I hadn't killed anyone, I felt my behavior was as bad as theirs—it was as if I could see through their eyes, in a way. I was on the same plane with them because they, too, were unable to control their behavior. I was afraid that someday my own actions would careen so far out of control that I would also become a murderer. What was there to guarantee I wouldn't? I thought I'd end up in a prison cell. I was terrified of my own feelings and temperament. Thinking about murderers also thrilled me because I knew they were worse off than I was; I was not living in a prison cell and they were!

He began asking "What if . . ." questions. What would happen if I threw this crayon into the dryer? What would happen if I poured water onto the stove? What would happen if I threw Meg's book out the window?

Though Ron and I didn't believe in any organized religion, we wanted to give our children the chance to make up their own minds about it in time, so we went to a number of churches in the area, trying to find one that was racially integrated. One Sunday we tried a large Presbyterian church. The four of us sat while the preacher droned interminably on and on, telling us about the true Christian spirit he had found aboard an aircraft carrier, that God was on the side of "our boys." We were seated in the front row of the balcony. Suddenly Sean stood up and leaned forward, peering over the railing. "What would happen if I jumped?" he asked loudly.

Ron yanked him back onto the seat. "You'd be killed!" Ron whispered to him.

"Then I'm jumping!" he shouted.

Ron took him outside to wait for Megan and me. Actually, we envied them both.

A couple of weeks later Ron and I were just waking up one morning when we saw Sean standing at the foot of our bed, staring at us. He had a strange look in his eyes. Was he sick? (It was always nearly impossible to tell until we saw some real symptoms.) Then he said, "What would happen if I poured gasoline on this bed and lit a match?"

His main interests now were license plates, rooftop television aerials and the direction they pointed (he would change the dial on my father's antenna and then charge outside so he could watch the aerial turn), and radio and TV station call letters. He'd given up his litany of state questions and replaced them with, "Do you get WOL? How about KDKA? KQN?" He knew thousands, remembering the information about where each was located and compiling it like a researcher on sheet after sheet of notebook paper, meticulously written, carefully kept in a box under his bed.

I loved the information I could obtain on radio and TV call letters—the letters themselves and the cities where they were located. It was easy to find the information since the stations were listed in National Geographic *magazine. I knew it was knowledge that few other people had, and that made me feel excited and powerful—so much so that I kept a list of the call letters in my head. On any given day one station's letters would stick in my mind, repeating themselves over and over. I'd use these repeating letters to shut out the people around me and all the things going on that I didn't like. The sound of the letters was strong and vivid, blotting out all my insecurities. I did this for many years and it always made me feel powerful. I was the only one in the entire school who had this information, and as long as the letters spoke in my head, I was no longer inferior.*

An extension of my fascination with call letters was seeing them on the television screen. When I was at my grandfather's house, I loved to change the TV aerial. It was thrilling because I knew all the stations he could possibly get in his area—their letters, locations, everything—so when I moved the needle the aerial rotated and another set of channels came in. All I wanted was to see the station identification letters, not any of the programs. Grandpa didn't like what I was doing, and he would get very angry. But since I wasn't doing it to make him mad, I did it anyhow. I just had to see what those call letters looked like. I traced the shapes of them onto notebook paper from the screen.

*   *   *

One afternoon, when he was nine, Sean took a survey at the public library where Megan and I got our weekly stack of books. I had left both kids downstairs in the children's library while I went up to the adult section. When I returned fifteen minutes later, the atmosphere in the room had altered drastically—the Ice Age had come. The few patrons who remained were huddled in the corners; the librarians moved papers about on their desks, reluctant to meet my eyes. Sean sat in the middle of the room alone, making little noises to himself under his breath, the type we could never quite hear well enough to understand. I gathered the kids' things and we left.

"What happened?" I asked Megan quietly. She would say only, "Sean used a bad word."

A librarian friend told me the story the next day. Sean had circulated through the room asking every child, every parent, and each librarian, "Do you, or any member of your family, use the word 'fuck'?"

He still disliked being touched, but he had devised a way, I believed, of using affection as a weapon. He'd do whatever he wanted to do all day while I yelled and fought him until I was so furious I could hardly look at him. Then someone would stop in to see us. In front of the visitor Sean would look me directly in the eye and say (in a poor imitation of Shirley Temple), "Mommy, give me a hug!" I'd have to do it—what kind of mother could refuse to hug her child? (with a witness)—although I'd want to shake him. There was never any affection in his body, and the look he gave me when I put my arms around him seemed to say, "I've won again."

*　　*　　*

Both Ron and I talked to Sean constantly, for years and years. We said everything we could think of, trying to use new words, clearer explanations, better examples for what we couldn't get him to understand. We fought with words against irrational, erratic, destructive, compulsive behavior and against our own rage. Regardless of how many times we corrected his behavior, the same thing would happen again. He would always get angry with us for interfering, as though we had absolutely no right to have any part in his life.

We hired a new baby-sitter—a sweet, born-again Christian teenager who was a student of Ron's. I guess we thought her compassion quotient might be higher than the norm; besides, we had run out of baby-sitters.

When we came home just before midnight, we found her in tears. "Look what he did!" she said, shoving her bible into Ron's hands. The inside cover and many of the margins were covered with obscenities in Sean's handwriting. We apologized, tried to explain that he hadn't really meant to be disrespectful to her or sacrilegious, that there were some problems . . .

Ron confronted Sean the next morning, telling him how angry he was, that he could not spend his life destroying things, paying no attention to other people. Sean didn't respond. Ron's anger flashed out of control, fueled by the accumulation of frustration and rage we both carried inside us, by his ongoing attempts to neutralize the antagonisms between Sean and me. Something snapped.

"You try to ruin everything—that's all you like to do. I'll show you that you're not the only person who can destroy things!" He ran to Sean's bookcase and shoved it over, spilling out the books. He yanked out the drawers of the dresser and flung the contents onto the floor. Sean, terrified and crying, screamed for him to stop. So did I, trying to put things back even as they hit the carpet, pleading for him to think about what he was doing. But there was no stopping him. He grabbed the curtains and ripped them from the windows, took the mattress from Sean's double bed in his arms and tossed it down. When there was nothing left to overturn, Ron walked out of the room.

————————

This baby-sitter was a new person and I wanted to do something to see her get mad—it was like a game; I just had fun doing it. I was only teasing her the way I teased the bees in our backyard, or my sister and my mother; it was the same thing. Whenever she was out of the living room, I sneaked down and wrote something in her bible. I wrote as much as I could and then ran upstairs before she saw me.

When Dad got mad I didn't connect what was happening to what I had done. I couldn't believe he would get so mad—I thought he would just reprimand me the way he usually did, and I was even looking forward to that in a way. (I liked to control people's reactions, and it made me laugh to see them do what I expected, especially my mom.) But it sure wasn't like that this time! Dad's reaction was way, way out of proportion to what I'd done, and I was terrified. He destroyed my own room right in front of me! I would have expected that kind of reaction from my mother, not from him, but even she had never done anything like this! I thought that when he'd ruined everything in my room then he would come after me. He didn't, but I got into my closet and shut the door and stayed there so that if he came back he wouldn't be able to find me. After a long time I crept out and started cleaning up my room.

I had to change—I had to! But I knew that once the fear wore off, the behavior would control me again. I knew the whirlpool was there, waiting to suck me into it, and I felt doomed.

Sometimes Ron and I were convinced that we were both insane—after all, it was hopeless, he would never understand, something was missing in him. We'd reach the point where we couldn't stand the sound of our own voices one more second, but still we kept on. Had we not, we would have had to admit that it was over, that we were giving up. There were those tiny moments, so rare that each time we were afraid it had been the last, when Sean's eyes registered a presence—we had a child who wore a mask, who was indeed a prisoner.

Ron and I talked to each other. Was he evil? Did he enjoy causing us and himself such pain? Or had he been treated with extreme negativity for so long now that it was the only kind of attention he wanted, the only kind he knew he could get?

Most of the time he was clearly controlled by his behavior, but there were those other times when he seemed to know exactly what he was doing. He'd wait to catch my eye, then walk up to Megan as she worked on her homework. Making sure I was watching, he would begin whispering into her ear, hissing like a snake, bumping her arm as she tried to write, snatching away the paper she was writing on. Other times he'd sneak into her room and take her favorite new book.

Megan was amazingly forgiving, though. A few minutes after she'd been yelling at him to leave her alone, the two of them would be sitting under the huge pine tree in the back yard, constructing towers out of mud cakes and sticks. Sometimes they made "secret" notebooks together—lists of games to play in the neighborhood, complete with maps. The games would last awhile, then the teasing would begin again.

Ron and I constantly discussed what to do. What was there that we had not yet tried? We had nothing to go on, since no method worked better than any other. We were haunted by the thought that there was something we'd overlooked, that if only we were better parents, we would have found it by now. I tried things I was sure would work, others that made no sense at all. I did anything I hadn't yet done. For a week I didn't talk to Sean at all, having decided that words were a waste, that I might reach him better with gestures and silence. In place of the words, I smiled. I made hand gestures and I smiled, touching him gently and reassuringly at every opportunity. I didn't correct him, didn't allow myself to look angry—of course, my feelings were another matter entirely—and pretended his behavior went unnoticed. He didn't care, though he pulled away when I touched him, and his repetitive activity increased. I went back to talking, to yelling. Had it been a stupid method or had I given up too soon?

For a while I corrected him in a whisper. I did not allow myself to raise my voice, to create the ugly atmosphere he and Megan were so used to. I was patient, I thought. I explained again and again what he couldn't do to reinforce the idea that it was what he *did*, not who he *was* that needed to change. We had always told him we loved him, incessantly, trying, again, to make him see that we disliked his *behavior*, not him. He didn't notice the distinction.

I realize that during most of my childhood I simply did not hear my mother. Her efforts to be patient and kind to me did not reach me—I paid no more attention to her words than I did to the sound of a car going down the street outside. Her voice was just background noise. Only when she started yelling did she get through to me, bringing me out of my shell temporarily.

I made charts when I stopped whispering. On large white paper I wrote down everything he did that we could praise. He brushed his teeth—I wrote it down. He ate dinner—the same. That was about it. He didn't look at it anyhow. After two weeks I took down the chart.

Mostly I kept yelling. No wonder he was fascinated with tornadoes—he talked about them, wrote stories about them, drew pictures of them. I knew he felt he lived inside one, a victim of forces he couldn't control.

Ron and I felt as if our lives were devoured by our son. We were battered parents. We had the sense, or the good fortune, never to blame each other. I needed Ron's support desperately, and I got it. I was only too aware of my own failings, Ron of his.

By the time Sean reached fourth grade and was ten years old, I believed I had lost our battle decisively. I was out of ideas, unable to think of anything we hadn't already tried. I was bored to death with the whole subject of what to do and in despair over my own lack of patience and my cruelty; I continued to behave in a way I knew full well was futile and destructive. I was convinced that I hated my son. Everybody, I told myself, has a certain amount of love, kindness, understanding. I had used mine up, there was no more; it had never been replenished and it was bone dry.

Sean had begun asking, "What would happen if I killed myself?" When it reached the point where I wanted to say, "Go ahead, but kill me first," we began looking once more for help.

Ron and I asked anyone we knew who might be able to give us a lead. Things had not changed much since we had first looked for help six years earlier—there were still no choices in the city where we lived. We were told about a new diagnostic center at Case Western Reserve University in Cleveland, a center where they would test Sean, observe him, then make a recommendation for further help.

We drove to Cleveland. Our appointment was with a psychologist whose field of expertise, she explained, was with "extreme temperaments," people with such heightened sensibilities that they could not adjust to the normal world. (Like Edgar Allan Poe? I wondered.)

Ron and I gave her background information on Sean, a summary of our ten years of trying unsuccessfully to learn how to live with him. She said that she wanted to see him alone, that she'd talk to him, do a psychological profile, then give us the results.

It took more than an hour. We sat and waited in silence. Once Sean burst out of the office and yelled, "I'm bored of this!" Reluctantly he allowed the psychologist to pull him back inside with her.

She gave us her diagnosis immediately. "He is very animistic," she began. "How much that affects the autism I don't know."

"Animistic?" Ron said. "Why do you think that?"

"His entire attention became focused on a fly that was buzzing around the room," she explained. "He couldn't take his eyes
off it, then he began talking to it—transferring his own personality onto the fly. He said things like, 'Bad fly, no one likes
you! You're a very, very bad fly!' and then he'd laugh. I had to
ask him over and over to do the simplest things, but he wouldn't
stop watching the fly. He evinces signs of extreme temperament
as well; he's quite poorly adjusted to reality."

Doubt roared through my head. Had this woman been an
expert in pyromania would she have found Sean a latent fire-
bug? Why did they all come up with a diagnosis within their
particular fields?

I said, "As far as I know, he has never transferred his personality to an insect before. Probably he's very nervous and
afraid, and for whatever reason he reacted that way. It certainly
isn't typical of him."

She looked at me skeptically. She had a recommendation to
make. "It's called Beechbrook and it's a residential school with a
staff of fully trained teachers and psychologists. Because it's part
of the Ohio public school system, Sean's own school will pay the
tuition, and your family's room and board fees will be based on
your income." She paused. "I think you should go and take a
look at it while you're here."

---

*That fly was stuck in the room with me and the strange woman. It
was trapped and wanted out, just like me. We had a common bond.
The strange woman talked and asked questions, but I paid very little
attention to her. I did not want to be there with her—what had I
done now and why was I being punished? I was being interrogated*

by another stranger. Part of me sensed that I was going to be sent away. Because we had driven so far from home, I felt they were getting ready to get rid of me. I was extremely anxious in that room. All I wanted was for us to go home; I wanted to start over, to change the way I acted, but I didn't know how.

Beechbrook wasn't far from the university, so we took her advice. A place we could actually afford sounded too good to be true. We drove across the snow-covered countryside, through some scattered small towns. Finally we came to the turnoff; the sign beside the road said, "Beechbrook—For Emotionally Disturbed Children." The words burned into me and my eyes filled with tears. We drove through the woods until we reached a cottagelike building that looked as if it had been built in the late 1800s. The setting was serene—eight acres of land, a creek winding through it, woods, and a number of cozy old Tudor-style buildings.

The three of us went first to the administration building to meet the woman who ran Beechbrook. She was hearty and affable. They would accept Sean, she told us, although he was close to the cutoff age—they handled kids between the ages of six and twelve. Still, she felt sure, he would benefit from being there for just the two years. He would live at Beechbrook during the week and go home with us on weekends. When we came to pick him up we would have family therapy sessions, all four of us. He would attend school every day, on the grounds, in classes with only six or seven other children, and he would be graded according to the regular public school system. Twice a week he would meet with his own therapist. They had an athletic program on the grounds; also the kids were often taken canoeing,

129

hiking, bowling, and to movies. They were given chores to do in their own residence to build responsibility.

As the director spoke, I watched Sean. He squirmed, fidgeted, looked around the room. He didn't appear to be listening.

She took us on a tour of the grounds and facilities. There was a recreation center, the school, a church, and three residence cottages; Sean would be assigned to one of them. We went inside and met the cottage leader, a gentle young man who lived with the kids he supervised. There were eight of them. They stared at us as we walked through, except for one, who lay facedown on the living room floor, slowly kicking his feet.

The cottage was drab and dingy. An atmosphere of hopelessness and desolation permeated the rooms, and signs of violence were everywhere—fist-sized holes in the bedroom walls, splits in doors, cracked and shattered mirrors, ripped upholstery. One could feel the rage that filled this place; surely the house couldn't contain it all! Some of these kids had been here for years, their childhoods swallowed up by the darkness of isolation. They had not chosen to be this way, but when they couldn't adjust to the world, they were cast out of it.

We walked back to the administration office. The director described the theories on which Beechbrook was run. The idea was to gather a whole picture of the child, so Sean's teachers, his therapist, his cottage leader, the cook, our family therapist—everyone who dealt in any way with our son—would pool their information, observations, and experiences in order to learn as much about him as possible; then they could suggest ways to help him and us.

Every six months there would be a meeting; Sean, Megan, Ron, and I would talk with the head therapist, a psychiatrist, and all the people involved with Sean. Together we would do an evaluation, noting problems and progress. In addition, since the school at Beechbrook was fully accredited, Sean would stay at grade level when he returned to his original school.

We drove the sixty-five miles home on that freezing January night without talking. There was nothing to say—we had no choice.

We sent Sean to Beechbrook the second week of February. We tried to pretend he was going off to camp, that it was an adventure. Ron sewed name tags into his clothes, and I shopped for the things he needed and packed them. We talked to him about the new school and what he'd do there. I asked how he felt about going. He didn't answer.

"Honey, we need a little time away from each other," I said. "We yell at you too much and we get too angry—the people there will talk to you and to us. They will help us and make things better, then we'll all be together again—very soon."

I told him about his therapist—that he would have a person he could say anything to—how angry he was with us, things he didn't like, and so on. It was safe, I kept insisting, for him to tell the therapist anything at all. Over and over I said that we loved him, that he would come home every weekend, that we would miss him very much. He didn't seem interested. Was he scared? I was afraid to ask him for fear I'd plant it in his mind if he wasn't.

I realized that semiconsciously I had expected a change in his behavior when he knew we'd decided to take this drastic step. I had hoped that something might click and he'd think—oh, my God, I've gone too far this time; I'd better stop it! Of course, no such thing happened.

She talked to me about going to that place. I'd be there for five days in a row—that was an eternity to me! The words were no comfort. I was scared as hell!

Megan, though she could barely tolerate his presence much of the time because of his incessant teasing and his destructiveness, had a much better relationship with Sean than we did. She had taught him to play checkers and Monopoly, and for at least a while could get him to stick to the rules; she invented games that incorporated his fixations with lists, with maps; she was amused by many of the things he said and did, things that drove me crazy. Despite his resentment and jealousy of her— the sister for whom everything was easy, who was never screamed at—there was an undeniable bond between them, a secret language only they understood. She seemed to know that he never really meant to do what he did, and she forgave him.

When we told her about Beechbrook she was furiously opposed to Sean's going there. We explained it to her, said it was only temporary, that we believed it would save us all, that we didn't know what else to do.

"You're sending him away. He'll hate that and be sad and lonely there." Her eight-year-old eyes filled with reproach, and she ran to her room, refusing to listen to our pleas for understanding, for forgiveness.

I watched Sean. I imagined calling the whole thing off, keeping him with us, going on as we always had. After all, we'd made it this far. It was impossible to reverse the tide. Mentally I was astonished that we were going through with this; emotionally I felt absolutely nothing. I remembered his birth, our son so full of promise, of unlimited potential. I dragged out every poignant memory of him I could. It was as though I were watching a slide show of somebody else's life. Something inside me has died, I thought. How long can a mother continue loving a child who doesn't love back, ever? A child who overtly rejects her love every time it's offered, year after year? For ten years Sean had been telling me: I don't like you, I don't need you—just get out of my way!

When the day came to take him, I couldn't go. We packed his things in his new suitcase, bought him a little bright-red rug to cheer up his room, filled his yellow footlocker—an attempt to hold off heartbreak with primary colors—and he and Ron got into the car. It would be worse if we all went anyway, I told myself—how awful to take him there and leave him and for all three of us to get back into the car and drive away. It's better to make it casual, just he and Ron should go. Meg and I will stay home as if it's no big thing.

We hugged him good-bye. "You'll have a good time there," Megan said softly. "They'll have lots of kids for you to play with. And we'll see you in only four days!"

We waved until the car disappeared. Megan and I stood silently for a few minutes before she went to her room and closed the door. I lay down on the couch. I had never felt such loss.

The sixty-five-mile-long car ride was endless. I was extremely apprehensive the whole time. I knew I was receiving the ultimate punishment—they were sending me away! I kept thinking, "This is it—it's all over for me now!" I felt I was damned.

I knew that for years my behavior had been deplorable. I was *always being yelled at for something. Now that I was ten years old I knew my parents hated me—they had to or they wouldn't scream so often. Up to this point I had always had my own safe haven—my home, my own room, my toys. Now I was being deprived of all my security. They were telling me that not only was I rotten, I also was no longer worthy of being part of this family.*

I had no idea what I had done to be sentenced to this punishment. I was bewildered, fearful, and angry. What had I done to throw them over the edge?

When my dad dropped me off it took awhile before the full reality of the situation set in: My God! Here I am alone in this strange, awful place. How long do I have to stay here? I saw right away that there were all kinds of kids around, none of whom I knew. I could also see that they were "odd," that each of them had something wrong and that they were not like normal kids. Since something was wrong with them, it was clear that something was also wrong with me or I wouldn't have been sent there.

I was told where I had to stay. It was a dingy, two-story house called Severance Cottage; it looked more than 100 years old. Someone showed me my room. Looking at it gave me a hopeless feeling; it was a prison without the bars. Though there was no steel door, it felt like a cell. I knew I was confined. If I tried to run away, I'd be brought back and punished somehow.

The day was endless. Finally, Ron came home, his eyes red, his face ashen. Wordlessly we held each other for a long time. At last Ron said, "When I left him he seemed okay—I don't think he noticed."

I lay awake most of the night. Images flashed through my mind of Sean lying alone in that strange bed, abandoned, surrounded by strangers. He would be cold, I knew, because he always kicked off his covers, and we always went in and covered him. I wanted to cry, but there were no tears.

In the next few days I realized more clearly than ever before how the life of our family centered around Sean's aberrant behavior; the extent to which he controlled us all was extraordinary. Who were we without him? I saw how Megan accommodated Ron and me by keeping her own problems to herself—so successfully that I nearly believed she *had* no problems—because she knew we already had all we could stand with Sean. Slowly the three of us began to expand—aware for the first time of just how much strain and tension we had been living with, had accepted as part of daily life.

I taught all week as if I were new at the job; I looked at my lesson plans as if someone else had made them out. Every morning as I dressed I thought I couldn't possibly face all those kids and their demands and their problems today! But I did, and the kids—their irrepressible high spirits, their good humor, their overwhelming immediacy—pulled me out of despair and kept me going.

At home, I was stunned with loss one minute, filled with elation and relief the next. Megan alternated between buoyant good spirits and melancholy. One night at dinner she said, "Do you think they'll give him good food? Will it be clean and everything?" When I put her to bed she said, "I wonder what he's doing right now at this second—do you think he's thinking about us, too?"

On Saturday morning the three of us went to Beechbrook. When I saw our son I felt as if I had been punched in the chest. He looked like an orphan—his shirt was buttoned wrong, both shoes were untied, his hair stuck up all over his head. I had always helped him dress, straightening things, fastening difficult buttons. I wrapped my arms around him and held him tightly against me. He stood perfectly still. "Sean, we've missed you so much! Are you okay?"

"Yes." Ron and Megan hugged him. He was subdued, his shoulders sagged. He looked smaller. Lost.

To make things even worse, we had to leave him at Beechbrook until Saturday, though all the other parents, who lived much closer than we did, came for their children on Friday night. The family therapist didn't want to stay until 8 o'clock at night for our session, and the hour-and-a-half drive meant we couldn't get there any earlier, so we'd agreed to wait until Saturday.

Our therapist was Dr. Borden, a small, plump woman in her late forties. Our session with her lasted an hour and consisted mostly of her gathering preliminary information. She asked questions, took notes, chain-smoked. Then at last we were free to take Sean home.

He and Megan talked to each other in the back seat. Both of them pretty much ignored us.

"Are they nice to you here?" she whispered.

"I don't know."

"What did you do this week?"

"I don't know."

"Do you like your teacher?"

"Yes."

When we got home he tore through the house, checking everything, making sure no changes had been made.

The weekend wasn't easy, despite my vows that it would all be different from our past life. As if he had been deprived of all his repetitious behavior for a week, which indeed perhaps he had, Sean did it all with a vengeance. I wanted to show him how much we had missed him, to be accepting, loving, but I found myself yelling again, even spanking him. Late the next day, when it was time to take him back, we felt abused, full of guilt, and overwhelmingly relieved.

When we reached Beechbrook Sean got out of the car and headed for his cottage without a backward look. It's obvious, I thought, that he's glad to get away from us. It's easier for him here than it is at home. He doesn't feel anything except rage and frustration toward us. It's better this way.

The rules at Beechbrook were very rigid—what time we were to be up in the morning, what time we were to go to bed, chores we were to do every day. Because it was so structured, it didn't take me long to know what was expected of me. However, I in no way felt secure or comfortable; I was always afraid. The only security I had was in the absolute regularity of things—our dinner was delivered every night at precisely six o'clock; we had waffles—my favorite—on Wednesdays.

The other kids made life miserable for me. Since I was already afraid of other people, I was really terrified of these kids because I had never even seen them before, and now I had to live in the same house with them! They all seemed very strange to me. One of them, Andrew, I tried like hell to avoid. He was two years younger than me, and smaller, but still he tormented me each time he saw me with punches and teasing.

I was so afraid that even though I tried to conceal my fear, the other kids saw it and were drawn to me as a victim. Almost all the other kids had at least one friend, but I had none and retreated even further into myself. I was scared to say anything to anybody about my life at Beechbrook.

Although I liked some of the off-grounds activities—like bowling, sleigh-riding, and going to the Dairy Queen—I hated having to go with the others. I felt as if I were being chased down a dark alley, running for my life, five days every week, with only two days of safety and tranquility at the end. I was so afraid that I would sit on the couch in the living room of the cottage pretending to watch TV just so I could blend in. Because I could see that all these kids were weird and even they didn't accept me, I knew I was the strangest one of all.

I devised my own kind of escape from the other kids. I had to have some control. The things I used at home—Tinker Toys, cards, crayons—weren't available to me, so I had to find substitutes. One escape was the box of Cream of Wheat stored in the pantry. Whenever I could, I sneaked into the kitchen and carefully tipped out a handful of the uncooked cereal into my palm. I ate it quickly, licking it off my hand. I loved the taste because it was perfectly bland.

Another activity I loved involved the washing machine, also located in the kitchen. The laundry was done in the evening, after dinner, and none of the staff was in the room while the machine was on. I would sneak into the kitchen just before the machine was about to enter the spin cycle. Since it wouldn't spin unless the lid was closed, I would rearrange the clothes so that they were off-balance, then run back into the living room before anyone noticed. I enjoyed this immensely and thought it hilarious when I succeeded. Off-balance, the washer made a loud, banging noise that could be heard by everyone in the next room. Of course, a staff person had to rush in and fix the clothes properly. I loved watching the staff person have to do this! I felt rewarded when I got away with it—which was most of the time—but I did get caught once or twice. When I did, it reinforced the other kids' notion that I was really strange. I did these things because I wanted to escape from reality and because they were intensely fascinating to me. I was not trying to cause trouble.

There was, though, one kid I enjoyed tormenting. Ernie was an eight-year-old who seemed harmless. He had a gaunt frame and severe speech impediments, and I thought he was somebody who couldn't hurt me; he seemed vulnerable. I liked to pick on him because of the way he acted when he got upset or angry, which was pretty often. He would stamp his feet and jump up and down, whining loudly before bursting into a full-fledged cry. This behavior was incredibly fascinating to me and very humorous. I'd sneak up on him when he was alone and pull his hair. The best time to do this was just after we got up in the mornings. I'd stay only long enough to watch his reaction, then I'd run down the stairs, slowing before I got to the kitchen so it wouldn't look like I had done anything wrong. I had to struggle to hold in my laughter so no one would be suspicious. Often he'd still be fussing when he reached the kitchen, but he never retaliated against me. Each time I succeeded—not only getting the response I wanted from Ernie but also getting away with it—I was quite happy, and my compulsion to do it more was fueled.

The desire to tease Ernie was like a physical presence inside me, pushing me to do it and blocking out the realization that I was hurting him. On the rare occasions when I was caught and someone brought to my attention the effects of my actions on Ernie, my desire was temporarily cooled, but only for a very short time. I quickly became filled with the desire to tease him again.

The next several weeks passed without much change. On the fourth Sunday we drove Sean back to Cleveland. I went to his room with him to put away his clean clothes. He paid no attention to me. I kissed him good-bye and went back to the car with Ron and Megan. As we drove down the long, circular road that went behind the buildings and then looped around in front of them, Sean burst out the front door of his cottage and raced down the hill toward us. He was screaming, "Stop! Take me too! Stop!"

In an instant we knew that if we did stop we would have to take him home, that we would have to give up Beechbrook and whatever promise it held out to us. We didn't stop. We drove on, all three of us crying. He ran after us to the edge of the woods and watched us drive away.

That changed everything. He did care; he did feel something for us—even if it was just homesickness. He didn't want to be left at Beechbrook—why had I been so stupid that I hadn't known? Or had I?

We talked about it at the next therapy session. "Are you angry with your parents for making you stay here?" asked Dr. Borden. Sean smiled distantly, looked away. He picked at a thread on the sofa he was standing behind. More talk. Suddenly Sean interrupted with a shout, "*No more! No more! I want to go on Friday, too. Do you hear me? No more!!!*

Dr. Borden changed our sessions to Friday night at 7:00. Sean had demanded he be allowed to leave Beechbrook when all the other kids did; we all agreed. But so far he hadn't insisted we take him home with us for good. Did that mean he simply did not have the ability to verbalize the desire? Or could it be that somehow he knew that staying at this place might help? Could it mean he forgave us?

Now, every Friday we left town the minute we all got home from school. Ron and I had taught all week and were worn out, faced with a weekend of paper grading and lesson plans. Our car was old and erratic, not safe to drive the three-hour round trip to Beechbrook and back through the snowbelt of Ohio. (Twice, in fact, the car did give out, and we had to phone for someone to drive up and rescue us.) When we reached the tiny village near Beechbrook we stopped for something quick and awful to eat and then, our hastily eaten food barely swallowed, it was on to family therapy.

The sessions were torture. Ron and I tried to be patient and reasonable with questions we found obvious in their intent and implications: The therapist was trying to ferret out what we had done to Sean and why. She knew we were the source of his problems, she just didn't know precisely how. I liked Dr. Borden; she was a kind woman and I knew she cared about Sean. But she was a follower of Freud, and Freudians knew what lay at the center of problems with children: the bad egg, the poisoned apple, *the mother!* If I was irritated, if I thought the questions were a waste of our time, she believed it was because I had something to hide.

Obediently, Ron and I talked about our own parents, our own childhoods. I tried to be interested; I wanted to scream and strangle Dr. Borden. "But we need *help*," I finally pleaded. "We need new ideas, positive methods, a program of some kind— something we can *do* to help Sean that we haven't already tried! We have every weekend to begin something new, and all we do is fall back into the old patterns, making all the old mistakes, reinforcing the negative behavior. Isn't there anything you can suggest!?"

"In time we will get to that, but for now all of this is important. We need to know more." And repeatedly she told us, "You have to accept that he can't change; you have to change around him, to learn to eliminate the conflicts."

"But how??"

"That is what we're trying to discover. Now, what were your feelings, Judy, when your brother was born?"

Megan and Sean hated every second of the therapy sessions. Moments after the hour began Megan would leap to her feet and say, "I have to use the bathroom!" "Me too!" Sean would say, following her out of the room. We could hear their laughter when they had safely reached the hall. If Ron or I didn't go after them, they never came back. They had to be hauled into the room, and then they refused to sit in the chairs; instead they stood behind them, fidgeting, restless, and as bored as we were. Sean focused on Borden's chain-smoking, staring at the smoke as it curled above her head. The room was tiny and airless, and the smoke irritated us all.

"Why do you smoke?" he suddenly asked her one night.

"It's a very bad habit of mine," she said. "It's something I shouldn't do."

"Then why do you do it if you know that?" Megan put in.

"Well, people have weaknesses."

We all thought our own thoughts in silence. Suddenly Sean grabbed the pack of cigarettes and examined it. With a deft twist of the wrist he tossed it into the wastebasket. Then he plucked the newly lighted cigarette from Dr. Borden's hand and squashed it out in the ashtray. After a second of stunned silence, Megan burst into laughter. So did Sean. Ron and I choked, tried to speak, then joined in the laughter. The session, only ten minutes old, was over. We couldn't control ourselves and, looking at us as if we were four incorrigible kids, Dr. Borden told us to go home.

*   *   *

What was it really like for Sean at Beechbrook? I tried, but failed, to find out. Trying to get him to talk about his real feelings was like pounding on a locked steel door. I asked questions; he spoke of zip codes and call letters. I knew it was all in there—the fear, the rage. But how could I break through?

Once, when he was nine, I had put him to bed and sat beside him, smoothing the hair off his forehead. Suddenly he fixed me with a strange look and said, "What kind of job am I ever going to get?" An electric current ran through me; my eyes filled with tears. I wrapped my arms around him and buried my face in his neck. "Any kind you want, honey—you'll be able to do whatever you want to do."

Now, for the hundredth time, I wondered if that had really happened. Could I have imagined it? But of course he had said it, he was capable of thinking it, and it showed there were fears and doubts that connected to the "real" world under all his compulsiveness. But how could I get him to trust me enough to talk to me, without numbers, states, letters?

The slice of my day that was least stressful for me was the school hours. Its structure gave me a respite from the rest of the chaotic, anxious day. For six hours the kids couldn't torment me, so I was relatively comfortable in the classroom. At first, being in a class with only seven or eight kids seemed weird to me after my class at Boardman, with thirty kids. And I deeply resented having to go to school at Beechbrook. I had loved my regular fourth-grade teacher; I had a rapport with her, she encouraged and praised me. So I was very angry that my parents had uprooted me and sent me away. What would the other kids think of my long absence? I couldn't say

I'd been sick all that time. I was infuriated with Mom and Dad for not waiting for summer to send me away!

There was something else that made Beechbrook even more difficult. There was a girl in my class at Boardman I was very attached to. I really loved her and wanted her for my girlfriend! Her name was Karen and she sat next to me. I kissed her several times. Once I dropped something on the floor, and when I bent down to pick it up, I kissed her shoe several times. When I looked up at her she was in a transition between a smile and real laughter. I got caught once or twice trying to kiss her when we were on the playground. She sensed how I felt. I knew she wasn't exactly in love with me. However, I could only wonder if and how her feelings for me would have grown had I been allowed more time with her. Then my own parents—the two people who were supposed to love me—caused me to lose Karen! My anger at Mom and Dad for destroying this relationship was immeasurable for a long, long time, but they never knew it.

I had no way of seeing Karen even when I went home for weekends because I didn't know where she lived. I couldn't write to her or talk to her. It was inconceivable that I could have looked her up in the phone book since I had no idea what a phone book was for. I did not solve problems of any kind. But I found a way of taking her with me. For several months I thought about her constantly. Often I talked to her before I went to bed, before I fell asleep. That was the only time I could be alone with her. The only trouble was that she never responded.

So the very year I thought I was making real progress in my class at Boardman, I was taken away and sent to a place as forbidding as Beechbrook. My parents had no right to do this to me! I never said a word to anyone about how I felt because I was powerless. I believed that Mom and Dad were so determined to send me away that nothing would change it, so why bother? I buried my enormous rage and hurt.

Not one day passed that I didn't wonder what the hell I was doing at Beechbrook. What behavior made them send me away? My life was filled with fear and desperation. I had to find my own ways of keeping my sanity.

One thing that amused me and gave me great pleasure was drawing tornadoes. The walls of my room were bleak and ugly; all I had to do was spend a few minutes in that room and my insides were shrouded in hopelessness. The room itself reinforced my feelings of powerlessness, so I decorated it by hanging up my pictures of tornadoes.

I was both fascinated and terrified of storms. First I would draw a serene landscape, then I'd add heavy clouds before coloring in the tornado funnel itself. Most of my pictures looked strikingly similar; it was the size or the shape of the funnel cloud that gave each one a separate identity. My pictures made the room look more cheerful to me, and I felt I was doing something important and productive to fill up the blocks of time that would otherwise have been wasted. I tried to make every picture look ominous and threatening. The drawings showed how I felt most of the time, and they were a release for my pent-up anger. I liked to draw a picture of Severance Cottage so that it was directly in the path of the savage tornado! I hoped that someone would come into my room and ask about the drawings so that I'd have a chance to express how angry I was, but no one ever did.

Our six-month evaluation at Beechbrook was at hand. We picked up Sean at his cottage, and the four of us went to the large conference room. Chairs had been set up in a circle around three sides of the room for the staff. There were four chairs in a line for us and a single chair in the center, facing us, for the head psychiatrist. We all went to our assigned places.

The psychiatrist, Dr. Russell, was short and roly-poly, with a round pink face and gray hair. I tried not to dislike him on sight. It was his show. He conducted the business at hand with pride and confidence—there would be no equivocating here! Most of the questions were directed at me, and he addressed me as "mother," sitting with his pudgy knees nearly touching mine. I moved back slightly and said, "My name is Judy." Looks were exchanged among the staff.

"How did you feel when you discovered you were pregnant?" he asked. "Did you want this child?"

I felt the heat of rage rising to my head. "Yes. I did want Sean. *I still do.*" I stared at him. His eyes shifted, and he smiled slightly at something just to the left of my ear.

"Ah, sometimes we think we want something we really don't want at all. Sometimes, you see, we are afraid of the truth."

There was a loud ringing in my ears. Suddenly his watch alarm went off and we both jumped. "Oh, sorry, I forgot to turn this thing off," he said, fussing with it. He glared at Megan and Sean, who were giggling.

He turned to the staff and asked for reports from the therapist, from Sean's teacher, from his house leader. Sean had been given chores in the kitchen—helping to mix pancake batter, taking out trash, washing dishes—because he had a rapport with the cook, Mrs. Leonard. Dr. Russell exploded.

"I will not have this! He is not to do anything in the kitchen—these are feminizing chores, and he is to be given a new assignment immediately!"

I seethed. I turned to look at Megan, whose eyes were wide with indignation. (Only a few days earlier, when she had finished reading all ten of the Carolyn Haywood *Betsy* books, she had said to me, "You know, the girls this author writes about do only uninteresting things like baking cookies and washing things, and the boys do all the building, playing, and having adventures. Too many books are this way!")

Dr. Russell was talking. He was telling us, but especially me, a parable. He was the star. He had been in the waiting room of an airport recently where a mother was trying unsuccessfully to quiet her crying baby. He observed her efforts. "She was doing everything right, but it just wasn't working."

His eyes swept the room. "I walked over to her and said, 'Excuse me. Do you mind if I try?' I took the baby from the mother's hands and held it to my chest. Instantly it became silent, content." He fastened his eyes on mine.

"It was no accident, you see. Whatever feelings were inside that mother were picked up by her baby—those feelings were *negative*, and crying was the infant's response to those negative feelings."

I heard a strangled half-laugh and realized I had made the sound. I shook my head in disbelief. Ron stood up.

"I have to put a stop to this," he said. "I cannot allow you to do this to my wife—you're trying to blame her, and we're not going on with this. We're leaving now."

Dr. Russell, his eyes a frozen blue, wrapped up the conference with a sentence about how good it had been to meet us and how pleased they were with Sean's progress at Beechbrook. I gathered up my shredded psyche, and the four of us drove home.

During the following therapy session we had a lot to talk

about. Dr. Borden implied that she was not in agreement with the psychiatrist's methods or his way of thinking, But *someone* is, I thought. After all, he is in charge of the place. Though Borden was a kind woman and well meaning, we never got over the feeling that family therapy was a punishment; that we were never going to get the help we so desperately needed.

The summer was lovely. Ron and I had Megan to ourselves, and we enjoyed every second of it. We swam, played tennis, rode our bikes, talked. We knew how essential it was for her to have time away from Sean. She needed the freedom to follow her own interests without being constantly interrupted by him or by our yelling at him. We all needed a respite from the storm of conflict that had enveloped our home for all these years.

Earlier that spring, Megan's third-grade teacher had asked Ron and me to come to school for a conference. She was, it turned out, very concerned about Megan's hearing problem and wanted us to sign a release to allow them to test her. What hearing problem? we asked.

She explained. As we knew, Megan was a great reader. There were many times, however, when the class bell rang and she never even looked up, other times when she would call Megan's name and she didn't notice. Instead, she simply continued to read. The teacher would have to go to her and touch her on the shoulder before she could get her attention.

"It's not poor hearing," I said. "It's good concentration. She concentrates so hard that she becomes unaware of her surroundings. Her hearing, actually, is quite acute."

The teacher and I exchanged a look. She understood. After

all, she had been Sean's teacher the year before, and her year-end note to us had read, "He has been the biggest challenge of my teaching career."

So the three of us had time to be together without strain and hysteria and screaming. We got more done than ever before—the yard was immaculate, I scraped and painted our house, we both painted Ron's mother's home. Yet we also felt lost, numb—with overwhelming guilt thrown in for good measure. We had cut off part of our family body, and the pain was always there.

School started again. Megan was in fourth grade, Sean in fifth. We resumed our old schedule of Friday-night therapy sessions, and they were worse than ever.

———

In September there were major changes at Beechbrook. For one, when the new set of kids arrived, some of the older ones got to leave forever. I also had to share my own room with another boy. It scared me to death having a roommate. Now I was going to be stripped of my privacy! I had at least been able to be alone whenever I wanted; now I couldn't even draw my tornado pictures and hang them on the wall with any assurance that they wouldn't be torn down.

My roommate, René Watts, was eight years old when he arrived at Severance Cottage that fall. He was tall and muscular, and his size alone was intimidating. For a short while I thought I would actually be able to come out of myself and befriend René, but that is not what happened.

He settled in at once. I had been at Beechbrook for seven months and I was nowhere near being used to it, but he seemed to feel at home right away. He was easygoing and seemed problem-free. I actually felt rather comfortable with him, and I began to loosen up—so much so that for the first time I began talking to another boy. When he responded, I let down my guard even more. Soon I actually found myself kidding around with him. My God, I thought, here's a person who is accepting me! It was too good to be true!

But like a car without brakes careening down a hill, the friendship was going too fast for me. I still wanted to be alone most of the time, and René wouldn't let me. He wanted me to take part in whatever he was involved with, even if I didn't want to. While I was desperate to blend in and keep out of sight, I couldn't do it when he was around. I couldn't avoid him because I had to share my room with him! I began to retreat, to pull back inside myself. I felt the way a turtle must feel when it pops its head out of its shell and someone grabs it. René became more and more insistent. He simply wouldn't leave me alone, and I wanted to scream! In no time I was a cornered criminal—I was trapped and had no escape. So much for making friends at that goddamn place!

I became completely withdrawn. All I wanted was for René to stay the hell away from me. I refused to do anything with him. No doubt he was still trying to be my friend, I see now, but I no longer allowed it. Soon, his offers of friendship turned into teasing. Though he was only eight years old and I was bigger than he was, I was afraid to do anything to him. I let him tease me mercilessly, and I did nothing to stop him. Of course, the problem was worse because I had to room with him every night. I couldn't take it! One day when I was home for the weekend, I whispered in Mom's ear, "I don't want to go back there again!" But they made me go anyway.

There was a staff person at Beechbrook named Sue Laine whom I absolutely refused to speak to. I pretended that she did not exist. The reason for this was that she was twenty-four years old, and I hated the number twenty-four—that was the number of the school bus at Boardman that was always late. It made me furious! Therefore, I ignored Sue Laine. Whenever she said hello to me I refused to answer her. Once she put her coat on a chair where I wanted to sit, so I threw it on the floor. She got quite angry with me for that—I had no idea why she should get mad, and I was shocked and hurt. I had expected her at least to ask me nicely not to do that, and I had planned to ignore her further. My refusal either to look at or speak to her continued all year. Just before the summer, though, she somehow got me to go for a walk around the cottage. She asked how I was getting along at the school. I gave one-word answers to her questions at first, but by the time we'd walked a while I had begun to open up slightly. I could sense genuine feeling coming from her. Then she told me she was leaving Beechbrook to work in Minnesota. I felt hurt and empty. I had just taken a big risk in trying to reach out to her, and then she had said she was going away! I'd been betrayed.

The rest of that year I pretended I didn't care a bit that she was leaving, but I did. I thought, there's nothing I can do about it, so I have to pretend it does not affect me in any way. It was another case of being separated from someone who really seemed to care about me, another kick in the face!

By October Sean had been at Beechbrook for eight months, and we couldn't stand it any longer. He was visibly unhappy, and one Sunday as we drove him back he said, "I hate it there. I want to come home."

Megan said, "I want him back so he can forgive us for sending him away. Can he come home before my birthday? That's all I want."

We brought up the subject at family therapy. The therapist said it was far too soon, that we couldn't interrupt a process we'd only begun, that it would do irreparable harm.

"We have to take that chance," Ron said. "We need him at home with us and he wants to be there."

"We all agree," Megan added.

We brought him home the first week of November. Megan had made him cards, drawings, and presents. We had bought gifts and we had a party for him. Megan told him, "We're going to have a wonderful time at home now, and you never, never have to leave again—not even for one day."

So what had we accomplished? Did nine months of separation do any good, or had we damaged him even more? Even now I don't know. It had given us time to heal, time for hope to grow again. We had come to realize that any answers we were likely to get would come from us, from struggling day after day with Sean and with ourselves. I'm still consumed with the question of whether or not I sent him to Beechbrook as a punishment, a lesson that would force him to see that there was a limit to what I could tolerate. When we had made the decision the winter before, my perspective was gone; I was a tangle of nerves, frustration, anger, and profound hurt. I felt worthless, a sham—how could I delude myself that I was a good mother to Megan when I was a terrible mother to Sean? I had no more resources, no more ideas, no more strength, and I no longer believed in the future.

———

They told me I was going home for good! I was filled with both relief and disbelief. I hated Beechbrook and couldn't wait to leave.

On the way home in the car I could feel the fear seeping out of me with every mile. *There was* so much *fear inside me!*

But when I got there I became terrified that if I screwed up, they would send me back. I really, really tried to control my behavior, but I still couldn't do it!

Sean rejoined his fifth-grade class, now in a much larger middle school a bus ride away. I had agonized over his having to go to a new school, after the term had already started, to a place where more mature behavior was required in a less insular setting—he now had a different teacher for each subject, the work was harder, the pressure greater, and letter grades were given.

Of course he didn't talk about it. No matter what I asked, and I did ask every question I could think of, I got only one-word answers or "I don't know." Do you like your teachers? Do you like the other kids? What subject do you like? He liked, he said, everything and everybody. (He never admitted disliking anyone until many years later.)

All I wanted was to get back into school, where I was supposed to be. I had a rule that I was to be at school for all nine months every year! I deeply resented that I had already missed two months. I was very embarrassed that I had been away, so I told the kids who asked that I had been sick.

When I saw Karen again, the girl I had loved the year before, it meant nothing. I was totally indifferent to her. The reason was that she now had braces on her teeth, and so I didn't want to look at her or to be around her.

Mom asked me a lot about school, but I couldn't answer, even when she talked to me in a very soothing way. When I thought of Mom I thought of punishment. So I figured that even if I could tell her about any problems, I would be punished in some way. I gave only quick answers so I could get off the hook—I didn't want to say the wrong thing! I didn't know which words led to bad reactions and which to good. Sometimes I told her I wished I had other parents— that if I did, I'd be happier!

As always at school, I felt a certain sense of security when I was in class. Any other place, however—the cafeteria, the playground, the halls—was a nightmare. I had no idea how to relate to other kids, and I spent my time fearing them. I couldn't understand why they behaved as they did or what their behavior meant.

Because I didn't act like them, the other kids teased me a lot. I tried to pretend that this never happened, to make believe I had no problems. So when Mom asked me what happened at school, I certainly didn't want to talk about what was going on—not to her and not to anyone else, either! I was glad my sister was still in our old school, because this way she couldn't see what was going on with me and tell anyone or talk to me about it. I needed to deny it to myself.

At home there was no improvement in Sean's behavior. All the same old obsessions were still there, with variations, and brand-new ones as well—all unstoppable. His fascination with light switches now extended to the neighbors. He went into their garages and flicked the outside lights on and off, lighting their driveways, their porches, their front and back yards. They often caught him, yelled at him, threatened, brought him home. Nothing stopped him.

He was still consumed with radio and TV call letters, with zip codes, washing machines, long words. If someone used a word he didn't know, he used it, too—with another meaning. I'd try and explain what it meant, gently. He'd yell, "I already know that!"

He teased the dog whenever he got it alone. He spent hours in the yard with the bees, kicking and swatting at them. Although he frequently got stung, it didn't faze him.

We bought him a bike for Christmas, the very first thing in his life he had ever asked for. He couldn't wait to ride it, yet he was absolutely terrified of it, of failing. Ron was determined to teach him. On the first clear day they took the bike to the school yard for space and privacy. Ron explained that it took time to learn, that he could take as long as he needed, that he could make as many mistakes as he wanted. Ron had him sit on the bike; he showed him how it worked, let him get comfortable on it. Ron held on and they moved forward. Sean wanted off. "I'm *never* going to learn!"

When they came home two hours later, Sean could ride his bike. Ron was limping from gashes on his ankles, and there were bruises on his arm. At the first fall Sean had panicked—he'd never learn, he was too stupid. Ron kept him on the bike, knowing that if Sean quit trying, he would never go back to it, that he would add this to what he thought was a towering list of his own failures. Ron held him on the seat, replaced his feet on the pedals. Sean took his hands off the handlebars; Ron put them back on. He took his feet off the pedals. Ron shouted, told him to keep his feet on and to steer the bike. Sean fought both the bike and Ron, falling a second time. Ron put him back on.

They tried again and again. Sean kept yelling, "I'm wrecking this bike—I want off it!" Ron struggled to hold the bike upright and Sean on it; when he moved it forward, the pedals gouged his ankles, but he didn't notice. Then the miraculous thing happened—Sean found his balance. He pedaled and began to steer. He rode away from Ron, who was running beside him, through the parking lot, with Ron calling out encouragement behind him. Half an hour later he rode home. He came into the driveway with a smile of such pride and delight on his face that I remember it to this day. Megan and I cheered, grabbed him, and hugged him. "Wow, Sean," said Megan, "you learned faster than I did! Now we can go everywhere!"

When the weather was good enough to play outside, Sean would join Megan and some neighborhood kids for a game, usually baseball. After only a few minutes, though, Sean would invariably leave the game to come inside. Meg and the others would protest, but he'd say, "I'm just getting a drink." Instead he would go up to his room until, tired of waiting, Megan would come in for him. "I'll be right down!" he'd call. "He's lying. Make him come out!" Megan would say. There was that telltale tone in his voice—he knew there weren't enough kids for a real game without him, so he would withdraw and watch their annoyance from the window on the stairs, chuckling to himself.

"Sean, go on out and play with the kids—they're waiting for you!"

"I'm too tired right now. I will after a little rest." A likely story. Of course he didn't, and the same thing was repeated the next time.

Then he developed the Fake Smile—a new method, I felt, to chip away at my tenuous grip on sanity. He would turn on me, and only me, a grin of such phoniness that I didn't know what to do. It was eerie—like some child-villain from a silent film contemplating his next victim.

And he patted me. He'd stand next to me as I graded papers, for instance, and begin patting me on the shoulder or arm.

Okay. I'd look at him and smile, maybe give him a hug. So perhaps it was the only way he knew to show affection, an awakening of an emotional response. The patting increased. Then the Fake Smile would appear. Faster and harder pats.

"Sean, why are you doing that?" Pat, pat, pat!

"I'm being nice."

"I see. Well, that's good. That's enough for now."

Pat, pat, pat, pat.

"Sean, please stop patting me."

"I'm just being nice."

"No, you're not. Do you think I'm a dog? Do you want to talk to me or something?"

The giggle. I'd grab his wrist to stop him. I was angry, and it was the reaction he was after; his eyes lit up as he tried to suppress his laughter. Why did I fall for it again? My reaction, I reminded myself, is my own choice. I have to stay neutral. I was the adult, goddammit, and he was the child!

After a few minutes the pats would begin again. I'd grab his hand to stop him. "Do you want to go for a walk?" He'd shake his head no, patting me with his free hand. I'd grab that one and hold them both. "Sit down here and tell me about school. What are you learning about in social studies class?"

"Nothing." Bright moist eyes, more pats. When I let go of his hands, he'd pat me again. I'd grab him, my fingernails digging into his wrist. He'd yank his hand away from me and throw himself onto the floor.

"Don't you hurt me!" he'd cry, a look of triumph in his eyes.

I believed that the only way to get attention from Mom was through any of several behaviors. If I did anything else, either Mom didn't say much to me or I felt totally ignored. One of the things I did was to give her a phony smile which was, I knew, completely transparent. I always did it to get a reaction from her—it was funniest to me when she returned the smile with the same exaggeration I had just given her, though I knew it made her mad.

I hardly ever really smiled, especially around her. Outside of my own repetitious behavior, almost nothing gave me real pleasure.

I started patting Mom as well as smiling. Even if I didn't feel any affection, I thought she would see that it meant I wanted to be happy. I was angry that I was angry, really, and I wanted all the fighting to stop. So the patting was sort of a way to break some of the tension, but the problem was that my compulsion made me unable to stop doing it. Mom got mad at me because I couldn't stop patting her. Sometimes I did it to tease her, but that was because my effort to be genuine had failed. Although I didn't feel genuine affection, I hoped she'd believe it was real, the kind Meg felt. I was afraid to hug her because I didn't know what she'd do—I couldn't understand the signs people used with one another. She didn't stay mad at me long when I patted her, though, and that fed my desire to do it even more. When she yelled I just ran away, then when she was over it, I'd come back and do it again.

If he had hated being sent to Beechbrook so much, why did he make no effort at all to behave better? Why wasn't he afraid we'd send him away again?

I tried to get Sean to help with work around the house. He was totally baffled by clothing and how it worked, needing help every morning with zippers, snaps and, especially, buttons. I attempted to have him hang up his shirts, but he slung them across a hanger, and when they fell off he became enraged, yelling at the rebellious shirts. Many of his clothes ended up in his wastebasket, ripped to pieces.

I insisted he make his bed in the morning and, when reminded repeatedly, he sometimes did, but it looked more disheveled afterward than it had when he crawled out of it.

I often tried to get him to help me rake the ever-present carpet of leaves, trying to turn a chore into a game by piling up leaves for him to dive into, but he'd last no more than ten minutes; then he'd throw down the rake and go inside, claiming he was too tired to do any more.

Although my grades were average or above, the rest of my school life was hell. At the age of twelve I couldn't relate to any of the other kids; I didn't know the first thing about them. I believed I was the only person who couldn't get along at home, that all the other students had good family relationships, since I never saw any other families firsthand. I felt radically different from everyone else. I stayed inside a shell of embarrassment throughout these years, and my feeling of shame was so enormous that I couldn't rise above it in order to befriend anyone. My own worthlessness overwhelmed me.

I spent an awful lot of time wishing I were a different person. Why couldn't I be normal? More than anything I wanted to change all my behavior and get rid of every problem I had. I started having "corrective" conversations with myself.

One day Mom asked me to help her rake leaves in our front yard. I deeply resented having to help her because of our bad relationship, so I always made excuses as to why I couldn't do what she asked. On this particular day I spoke in my monotone voice to Mom and told her I was too tired to rake leaves. She persisted. Then I said I wasn't feeling well right then. She got impatient with me, which made me

*want to help her even less. She said, "Fine. I'll do it myself. You
never want to do a damn thing with me!"*

I was deeply hurt by her reaction because, after all, I wasn't
trying to hurt her! I went to my room and watched through the
window while she arduously raked the piles of leaves. As I watched,
I had a conversation with myself. I divided into two people, one of
whom was furious with the "real" me:

"Goddamit, Sean—why do you make everybody mad at you?"

"Well, I only wanted . . ."

"You know better than to piss Mom off like you do! Everything
you do makes someone angry!"

"But I can't help it—I can't control my behavior!"

"Bullshit you can't! You're such a wretch! (Mom had called me
that when she was furious with me.) You better shape up!"

"Okay, so I have to change—but how?"

"I don't know how, but you better do it or they'll hate you
forever!"

"I'll try."

With this pledge I left my room and forced myself to be in a
different frame of mind. I joined Mom and started to rake leaves as if
the angry episode of a few minutes earlier had never happened. She
even smiled at me!

These conversations with myself provided a glimpse of the outside
world. I wanted to come out of my windowless cell and no longer be
a prisoner of habit.

Another method I used to deal with behavior I didn't want was to
address myself in the third person. When I was corrected for something I would usually say, "Sean, you know you're not supposed to
do that!" When I said this I could hear condescension in my own

voice. It annoyed Mom when I said this, and I don't think she knew why I was doing it. It was simply an escape—it removed me from my actions *and allowed me to sidestep the embarrassment. It let me off the hook!*

Also, as a way of making myself feel better, deflecting anger away from me onto someone else, I would tease Megan nonstop until she ran into her room furious and in tears. Mom would punish me, usually by sending me to my room. After I had had a chance to cool down, Mom would take me aside and try to get me to see the effects that my constant teasing had on Megan and on all of us. She'd say, "Sean, you've got to stop teasing your sister—she can't stand it!"

"I know. I really hate it when I tease her," I'd reply. "I'm the worst boy in the world."

Mom would look at me, puzzled. "Then why do you do it? It's like saying you hate to eat chicken and then wanting it for dinner every night."

The truth was I was on a merry-go-round and didn't know how to get off.

Sean was nearing adolescence, and Ron and I were afraid he'd never learn to do any of the things that would allow him to function as an adult. For the first time he was becoming aware of how much he didn't know and couldn't do. He was ashamed of his ignorance and did everything he could to cover it up. He lied, pretended to know what he was doing, said totally irrelevant things in order to ignore situations he couldn't face. He never asked for help and refused it when it was offered.

His fear of failing kept him from trying new things, from allowing himself to make mistakes until he learned a new skill. When he was twelve he said, "I need to play the piano now." We were thrilled. We found him a teacher, but he was constantly frustrated, dissatisfied with his own progress. He wanted to *play*, not to *learn* to play. "I should be good at this!" he'd cry out. "Other people are good, so I should be too!"

———————

I had heard Mom and Dad play duets on the piano, so I decided that I wanted to play the piano, too. I knew it would be easy and thought I'd be very good at it—I was sure I could master it.

When my lessons started I didn't like doing the boring, dumb exercises. All I wanted was to play and play well immediately, so I could begin impressing people. The practice books just got in my way.

Mom kept telling me that everybody had to learn an instrument slowly, that they all made mistakes while they were learning, and even when they knew how to play, but what she said didn't mean anything to me—I couldn't imagine that because I didn't actually see anyone doing it. All I saw was people playing flawlessly, so that was my rule—I had to play flawlessly, too!

At my lessons I got furious when I made mistakes; I couldn't tolerate that. Between lessons, I didn't practice. When they told me I had to practice to get better, it made me want to do it even less. It was a simple thing—I had to be a great player.

In 1974, the summer before Sean was to enter seventh grade, I heard about a newly formed group in Youngstown—mothers of children with learning disabilities. Not parents, I noticed; mothers. It was the first group of its kind in the city. Since Sean's behavior fit loosely into the description of learning disabilities, I was eager to find out if the group could help us. A friend and I went to the next meeting, held in the home of one of the organizers.

As we walked in I scanned the faces; there were a dozen women seated around the room. No one was talking and everyone looked anxious. The meeting got underway with a speaker, a psychologist from a clinic in the area. She talked for a few minutes about common behavioral problems of children with learning disabilities. Suddenly one of the women interrupted.

"My son is five years old and I can't toilet train him! They tell me he's retarded, but shouldn't he be able to learn at least that much?"

Another woman spoke up. "What about manners? Robbie refuses to eat with a fork, and the teachers complain that he throws food in the cafeteria. He's in Special Ed, so can't they get him to eat right?"

The speech was over, as far as these women were concerned. They wanted to talk. They needed help, encouragement, approval, instead of condemnation. They were women whose children's problems included everything from retardation to schizophrenia to cerebral palsy—everything except autism, so to my ears their problems sounded almost simple—no one even came close to describing the relentless behavior our son suffered from.

When the meeting was over I asked the psychologist if she had any experience with autistic children. "Oh no," she said, "and this group won't help you there. But I do know of a doctor who treats kids like that." She handed me her card. "Call me at my office and I'll give you his phone number. His name is Logan; the only thing is, he's located in Akron."

I searched continually for more information. I found a wonderful book called *The Siege,* another account of an autistic child, written by her mother. This little girl, unlike Sean, was withdrawn, quiet, easily "managed," but her behavior was only too familiar—the meaningless repetition, the fascination with lights, chains, running water. Not knowing where to go for help, the mother had relied on her own instincts and love, working with the child at home, trying with patience and ingenuity to lead her daughter into the world. At one point the parents took her to a famous school for a psychiatric diagnosis. Instead of being met with sympathetic people who gave them "reassurance and a little recognition, a little praise," they found the staff rigid and passive, refusing to respond in any way as the woman and her husband talked about their child. The author writes: "In the best of circumstances one cannot talk naturally to a listener who makes no response. . . . Here we were on trial."[4] And she adds: "We were controlled; we had no alternative. Refrigerator professionals create refrigerator parents. I had gone in in a highly emotional state, ready to tremble, to weep. Received with no reaction at all, I of course dried up my emotions and met professionalism with professionalism."[5]

Dr. Logan's face came back to me—his cold stare, his refusal to react, even to smile, as Ron and I went over the painful territory of our son's problems, stumbling over our confusion and fear. Yes, I thought, we had been on trial.

In the other books and articles I read, it was clear that there was still no agreement on the causes or treatment of autism. One thing I did learn was how lucky we were. Sean's condition could have been so much worse than it was—many autistic kids never spoke; often they banged their heads, bit their own hands, or were brutally aggressive to those around them. A majority were also mentally retarded, and for most of these children there was no hope but an institution.

Just when we thought we were through looking for outside help—that we had put Sean and ourselves through the evaluation/diagnosis/treatment mill for the last time—we got hooked again. Important new information on megavitamins and food allergies was being discussed in every magazine and newspaper I picked up. The latest nutritional theory, brutally abbreviated, was that children's behavior, particularly hyperactivity, is affected by allergic reactions to what they eat and drink. Doctors reported miraculous results with highly antisocial and uncontrollable kids who had been mistakenly thought brain damaged but who were merely the victims of chemical imbalances caused by food allergies. One expert specifically recommended that autistic children be put on a gluten-free diet. Since Sean's bizarre diet had been grain-based and therefore gluten concentrated since birth, I had to find out if his behavior had anything to do with food allergies.

We found a disciple of the leading expert in the field practicing in—of all places—Akron, Ohio! We took Sean to see her. Her office was in her home, a gloomy old place not much different from Dr. Rossi's. We were taken aback by her appearance—she looked much more like a palm reader/advisor than a nutritionist. She had dark, brooding eyes and long black hair and wore layers and layers of filmy printed clothing. She also had an observer at her side (a disciple of her own?), a dark, ominous-looking Russian man who muttered to her and said nothing whatever to us.

While Sean waited in another room, we answered her questions, tramping once more over the packed earth of our family problems, his autism and our inability to handle it. She had a questionnaire that she wanted Sean to answer, not us. She summoned him.

"Your weight, Sean?"

"Eighty pounds." (He weighed 103.)

"Your age?"

"Ten." (Of course he was twelve.)

"And how tall are you?"

"I'm 4 feet 8 inches."

I looked from our 5-feet-4-inch son to this woman taking down his answers. There was no expression on her face. Well then, I thought, she's being clever and registering his low self-image.

"What are your favorite foods?"

"Oh just about everything. I eat lots of fruit and vegetables. I'd say I eat balanced meals from the four main food groups."

What!? Ron and I smiled at each other. Our son who had never in his life allowed fruit or vegetables to approach his lips.

"Any foods you don't like?"

"No, none I can think of."

"What do you like to do?"

"I like to play all the main sports. I read a lot."

It went on. How on earth, I wondered, amazed, does he know how to create the perfect profile of the ideal twelve-year old?

When she was through with her questions and had taken a tuft of Sean's hair, she stood up and shook our hands. "I'll make an appointment for you in two weeks. By then I will have his program drawn up, based on this (she waved the questionnaire) and his hair analysis."

Ron was staring at her in disbelief. "Sean, will you go outside and wait for us on the porch?" When he was gone, Ron said, "Now wait a minute—are you using the information he just gave you for his program?"

"Well, of course." She looked baffled. "Is there some problem with it?"

"Yes. It's all lies, for one thing."

"Lies?"

"He gave you what you wanted to hear!" I said. "Can't you see by looking at him that he's eight inches taller than he said he was? And he's twelve, not ten. And all that about what he eats—his diet consists only of starch and carbohydrates; he eats huge quantities of bland food, nothing fresh."

She narrowed her eyes and looked at Ron, then back at me. "But why would he do such a thing?"

"Because he's a child with severe problems," Ron said. "Because he can't tolerate change, he's terrified of growing up. Because, as we told you, he's autistic!"

She stared at us. Her disciple stared at us. "Well then you'll have to answer this correctly for me or I won't be able to derive an accurate nutritional program for him."

And the amazing thing is, we did.

We went back in two weeks, listened to a list of his nutritional imbalances, bought the expensive minerals, vitamins, and food supplements that would solve all the problems. We talked to the guidance counselor at Sean's school, who agreed to make sure Sean took his twenty-six capsules every day at lunch. We gave him the rest of them—twenty-three—at home after dinner.

He hated taking the pills but he tried to cooperate. It was an awful thing to watch—some of the capsules were huge, most of them smelled terrible. But it's not drugs, I told myself; no tranquilizers this time! And there's a chance that if there really is a chemical imbalance that's making him do what he does, he'll begin to show marked improvement.

In a month we went back to our advisor/nutritionist. I had made note of minute changes in Sean's behavior to tell her about, changes that just might signal great results to come. She listened to the information as though unsure why I was telling her these things.

"Well, continue the program," she said abruptly, handing me a sheet with a name at the top, a name not Sean's, and a checked list of vitamins and minerals.

"This isn't his," I said.

She looked at me, her heavy eyebrows raised.

"This is someone else's program, not our son's."

She took it back and looked at it. "What is your son's name again?"

"Sean. Barron."

"And what has he been taking?"

My veneer of hope bubbled and evaporated, leaving me sitting in the chair with nothing but the usual emptiness and defeat. It was our final trip to Akron.

Ron and I made a decision. For better or worse, we were going to depend on ourselves from now on. We'd fight for Sean our way, and if we were wrong, the mistakes would be ours. We couldn't bear to raise our hopes again by taking him to one more professional and encountering yet another dead end. Not once had we been met with sympathy, compassion, or warmth; each experience had been devastating in its own way. And Sean did not need to be the object of another experiment. *"I'm not sick!!!"* he had screamed one day as he sat facing twenty-seven vitamins and minerals he was supposed to swallow.

During sixth and seventh grades Sean often returned from school visibly upset. Many times he had scratches all over his hands and arms. Had he done it to himself or was it another student? He pretended there were no scratches, that he had no idea what I was talking about.

"Tell me what's wrong, please, honey. Did somebody hurt you? I can see you're upset—are you having a problem with one of your teachers or is it the kids? Whatever it is, you can tell me—Dad and I will help you. No one will get angry with you." He wouldn't answer.

He wanted to ask questions, not answer them. They were the same questions, over and over. What would happen if I plugged up the bee hive? What will Meg do if I rip up her homework? Where does the Mississippi River go? He'd laugh whenever someone obliged and answered him, then he'd ask more. I believed he laughed because he had made the other person do exactly what he wanted, and it made me furious.

He began to say, "I hate it when you get angry! Don't do that again!"

I'd hold his shoulders and force him to look at me. "Sean, do not ask me that question again. If you do I will get angry." It didn't stop him.

———

When I was in seventh grade, I fell in love. She was in one of my classes—in fact she was the teacher, Miss Jenkins. From the first day

173

on, my feelings intensified, especially since I knew she wasn't married. I wasn't very interested in the science class she taught, and I didn't learn a lot about metamorphic rocks, but I couldn't wait for her class to roll around.

I felt that I had a special bond with her and that she didn't have such strong feelings for anyone else in her class—in fact, I was the only one who knew her first name! However, I was very worried that someone would find out about my feelings for her. I visited her every day before getting on the bus, and I was extremely angry and jealous if any other students were in the room as well. One day I waited so long to see her that I missed my bus and Mom had to come to school to pick me up.

Then a terrible thing happened! Miss Jenkins announced that she would be taking a week off to get married! A wave of panic and hurt spread through me, and I was drowned with pain. Everything I had spent months building up was washed out to sea. I knew my feelings would never be returned—she had betrayed me!

When she returned to school a married woman, I was sullen and bitter around her. One afternoon she was supervising my study hall. I was in a terrible mood and was withdrawn from everyone. I was completely nonresponsive and ignored everything she told me to do. For the first time all year, she yelled at me. It shook me and a heavy cloud of hurt hung over me for the rest of the day.

When I came back to school the following year she was gone, and I didn't miss her one bit.

At fourteen, for the first time in his life, Sean seemed to have a growing sense of himself. It was as if he, too, had become aware of another child locked within him, a "good" child.

"Sean, you just knocked over the clothes basket. Don't leave everything on the floor—pick it up and put it back into the basket."

"I did not *mean* to do it." He gave me a withering glance as though I had misunderstood him on purpose. "I am a very nice person. I never mean to hurt anybody!"

He'd tease Megan by reciting every word of a TV commercial into her ear twenty-five times until she ran from the room.

"Why are you doing that to her? I hate it when you tease your sister!"

"So do I. I hate it!"

"Then why not stop? That's all you have to do. You're the only one who can control what you do!"

But of course he had no control.

My mother was still Sean's refuge, and he spent as much time as he could with her. Several years before, she had resigned from her teaching job because of an illness that had begun as an infection and developed into what her doctor called auto-hemolytic anemia, a disease very similar to leukemia. She had always been extremely active, constantly moving, doing, never sitting still for more than a few minutes at a time. Now she had become a semi-invalid, living with pain, unable even to lie down comfortably, conserving her limited energy and strength. But her spirit was buoyant. She was uncomplaining and she chuckled at her own clumsiness, gently mocked her growing disabilities.

Since she had more time, she gave much of her attention to Sean. I drove him to her house after school several days a week, and the two of them spent the afternoons together. They played cards and games, and she had him help her with chores around the house that had become too difficult for her. Even with her, though, his obsessions took over when she wasn't watching him closely. He rotated the television antenna and ran outside to watch it move; he tossed whatever he could into the clothes chute and listened to the box, can, or toy crash to the bottom; he rolled marbles under the furniture and down the registers. My father found playing cards in the washing machine, toys stuck in the bushes, silverware in the rain gutters.

Sometimes when we arrived to pick him up, it was clear that his behavior had been a severe trial to my mother. The look of profound sadness on her face would fill me with despair. "He didn't listen today," she'd say. "I had to give him a tap on the bottom, didn't I, Sean?" For her, having reared two children whom she had never spanked, that "tap" was a major event.

In February 1976 my mother died. Apart from my own grief, I couldn't imagine the effect losing her would have on Sean. I had explained to him that her illness was serious, that she was growing sicker and sicker. He could see that she was weaker every time he saw her, but the last days in the hospital he had been unable to see her at all. He didn't ask about her condition; he said repeatedly, "She's getting better now and she's stronger every day!"

When I told him it was over, his face was like a mask. I held him for a long time, but his body was wooden, stiff. I searched for words to comfort him, but there was no comfort. He didn't cry, he simply turned and walked away. I felt responsible, deeply guilty. He would far rather, I knew, have lost me.

My grandmother died, the only person in my life I felt close to. I think I knew she wasn't going to get any better, but I didn't think she would die for years. I should have behaved better with her than I did.

I loved to help her around the house, and she was too sick to do many things herself. But then, after I'd scrubbed the kitchen or swept the porch, I'd feel like a victim of my own generosity. Even though I'd offered to help, I'd think that she only wanted me there because of the work I'd done. At the same time I knew this wasn't true, so I'd get angry with myself and take it out on her.

One day I was helping her burn newspapers in the cellar fireplace, and I got very angry. I yelled, "You only want me to work for you!" She was very hurt by my words and sat down without saying anything. I stormed up the stairs, turned off the cellar light, and slammed the door shut, leaving her there alone in the dark.

After several minutes I opened the door and went back down the stairs. She was still sitting there, staring straight ahead. She had tears in her eyes.

Now, at her funeral, I felt hopeless, filled with dread. I was the only one who had lost everything. My parents had each other; Meg had Mom and Dad who loved her, all the relatives had someone who cared for them, but I had nothing. My entire universe had caved in. Any chance of happiness for me went into the casket with my grandmother.

I knew I'd never see Gram again, and I realized for the first time that I loved her, that I had loved her for a long time. But now I could never tell her.

"I need to get a sense of humor."

"What?"

"You heard me. I need to get a sense of humor. Right now."

"But why, Sean?"

"Because every single person in the world has one except me. And I swear that nothing can stop me from getting one!"

He took joke books out of the library. "Why is this funny?" I read the joke he held out to me.

"Well, it's sort of hard to explain." Like impossible.

"But I *need* to know!"

I tried to explain. He watched me earnestly, uncomprehending. "But why is it funny?"

Taking a leap of faith, he repeated jokes to the neighborhood kids. They didn't know they were jokes.

"Mom, how do I get a sense of humor?!"

"I don't know, really. It's not something you 'get'—but you're fine the way you are; don't worry about it."

He worried. He gave up trying to figure out the joke books and started watching "Gilligan's Island" every day after school. It was the only television program he'd ever watched except game shows, which attracted him because of the flashing lights and repetitive noises. "But oh God, why did he have to pick 'Gilligan's Island?'" we all wondered. He memorized whole chunks of dialogue and repeated them to Megan.

"Why doesn't she laugh?"

"Because it's not funny like that, when it's not in the show."

"Yes it is. The audience laughed."

"I know, but that show has a laugh track—they just play a tape recording of people laughing." He stared at me.

"No," he said. "That is a very, very funny show."

"I'm glad you like it."

"Don't you think it's funny?"

"No, but different people laugh at different things—people see things different ways."

"I don't like that. I want to laugh at what *you* think is funny."

178

But he stuck with "Gilligan's Island." He remembered the "laugh" lines and repeated them to Megan, over and over and over, until she screamed with fury. I told him he had to stop. "She won't laugh."

"Sean, you can't *make* someone laugh if they don't think there's anything funny. When you repeat it, she thinks it's even less funny."

He used lines from the show at random, furious if we all didn't burst into guffaws, and he teased Megan mercilessly when she didn't respond. I told him that he had to stop teasing her or he could no longer watch the TV show. He kept on repeating the same lines over and over, to Megan and then to me.

"Okay, that's it. You can't watch that show anymore."

He argued violently. "You can't *do* that! Oh no you don't!" I said I had warned him many times and that I wanted to hear no more about it.

The next day he came home from school and, at 4:00, when "Gilligan's Island" was telecast, he sat in front of the television set without turning it on. For a half hour he watched the blank screen, chuckling to himself from time to time, sometimes laughing out loud. At 4:30 he got up. "Boy, that was a really funny show today!" he said as he passed me. I felt a chill pass over my heart. It's hopeless, I thought.

Every day for a month or so he spent that half hour watching nothing. Then (his position established?, his rage at my power over him assuaged?, his defiance cooled?) he stopped.

---

*I*n eighth grade I was faced with real trauma. I had no idea how to make friends or to fit in with the other kids at school. There was a new sophistication in the way they teased me—I would find my name scrawled next to some obscenity on one of the pages of a textbook; name-calling turned to practical jokes. The worse thing was never knowing whom I could trust or when I could trust them. I know now that the way I behaved made everything worse, but I didn't know it at the time, and I couldn't help it.

I loved to mimic certain TV commercials and programs to excess. I was also experiencing a resurgence of my desire to drop things on the floor, so I spent a lot of time dropping pens and pencils in class, getting yelled at for it, and generally attracting attention to myself— though not the kind I wanted.

The TV show that I copied most was "Gilligan's Island." Sometimes I'd recite a whole scene word for word. It was a repetitive show, easy to follow, predictable, and a comedy.

I had decided that I needed to get a sense of humor; I deeply resented the fact that everyone else seemed to have one. I believed that the more I watched "Gilligan's Island," and the more I memorized various episodes, the more polished my own humor would become. Every day I arrived home, rushed in, and turned on the show. It didn't matter how many times I'd already seen a particular episode—I'd watch it for the fourth time with just as much enjoyment as I had the first. I'd take the scene or two that I thought were most hilarious and play them over and over in my head. I would try to capture each nuance and then imitate it. When the actors said or did something funny, they always got laughs. Therefore, I concluded, if I did the same things, I'd get the same results.

The next day I'd have even more material to make the other students laugh. I wanted to win them over to me. However, my attempts at humor seemed to annoy them more than anything else. They reacted with irritation and I got increasingly angry and embar-

rassed. My anger extended to the actors on the show as well. "They drew laughter, dammit—so why can't I?!!"

My resentment of Mom shot sky-high when she forbade me to watch "Gilligan's Island" anymore. *It told me only one thing: Not only did Mom not find me funny, she was even punishing my attempt to gain a solid sense of humor! My rage and my desire to get even doubled.*

She even tried to get me to do something else during the time when I should have been watching my TV show! *There were to be no interruptions between 4:00 and 4:30!*

After she banned my program, I came home and watched the blank TV screen anyway. I gazed at it steadily even though it wasn't on. I simulated the laughter by giggling intermittently. I wasn't about to let her think she had the upper hand—besides, as I now see, it was a very good way to express some of the anger I felt without having to confront the issue squarely.

I also related to a few other shows that offered me comedy, shows like "Gomer Pyle" and "Green Acres." I watched them in the hope that I would get more ideas as I tried desperately to be a funny person. The kids at school did laugh when I repeated a line from one of these shows, but now I knew they were laughing at the strangeness of the way I was behaving, not at the humor.

For the first time in my life I realized that what I found to be funny wasn't "normal." Most of the things I laughed at and derived great pleasure from—things like teasing the bees and asking my repetitive questions—were just not pleasing or funny to anyone else. In fact, they made other people angry, made them think I was quite strange. All I wanted was to be like the other kids my age. It felt as if I was weird and strange on the outside, but inside I wasn't like that. The inside person wanted to get out and break free of all the behaviors that I was a slave to and couldn't stop.

At this time I had no ability to express my feelings with words. The thought never crossed my mind that I could ask Mom why I was so strange, that I could tell her I needed help. I had no idea that words could be used in this way. Language to me was simply an extension of my compulsions—a tool to use for my own repetitious behavior.

Things got even worse at school. Sean's pent-up rage when he came in the door every afternoon was palpable. As always, he refused to tell me what the problems were, though he did a lot of muttering under his breath, and once in a while we caught a name or two.

Megan, now in the same school with Sean, said that the kids on the bus teased him, and that because he had no idea how to respond to them, they teased him even more. He said bizarre things to his tormentors that made them sure he was crazy.

He hated the fact that his bus was the second one to appear in the school parking lot every afternoon. "It should be the *last!*" he told me. He didn't know why, he said, when I asked; it was simply his rule. So he stayed at his locker, pretending to be looking for something, until he could be the last one to board the bus. Time after time the driver had to wait after school for him, making the other kids furious.

Megan told him, "Everybody knows what you're doing, and they're mad at you for making them wait—they all want to go home! What you're doing doesn't make any sense, and it makes them think you're weird. Please don't do it any more!" But he wouldn't stop. He ignored her.

Megan usually did not confront Sean with his behavior because, as she said, it just didn't do any good. Now, though, she had begun to feel that he could control what he did to some extent, that he could be reasoned with.

I suffered tremendously at school. I was tormented, teased, and jeered at. The weight on my shoulders grew heavier with each passing year.

Since the pressure to conform to certain ways of doing things was so intense—and I could not get myself to follow the norms—I developed my own defenses. One of these was pretending to be a bus.

Like each of the buses parked outside the school, I had my own route. The hallways were my roads, and I worked out my route and followed it precisely every single day. I needed to feel in control; I despised my school bus for consistently being one of the first to arrive, for controlling me, so I adopted a route through the halls that meant I'd be the last person to get wherever I was going. This method helped counteract my anger and helplessness—feelings I always got when I looked outside and saw my bus already sitting there ten minutes before dismissal!

Twice each day I followed my route, making sure I was always the very last person to get on the bus in the afternoons.

In the mornings I went to my locker; then I began my route from there—walking to different set points in the halls and stopping at each one for a few seconds, the way a bus stops to pick up kids. By the time I completed my trek it would be almost 8:50 A.M., when the tardy bell rang. I made sure I got to my homeroom just before the bell rang so that I wouldn't call attention to myself by being late, but at the same time, I would be the last one in. I thrilled to see my desk the only one empty—it was a substitute for never getting to see the parking lot with the space for my school bus empty.

During lunch I did the same thing. I managed to arrive at the cafeteria among the very last kids. Sometimes the doors would be closed already, but I didn't care. Missing lunch was a small price to pay for being able to go on my journey through the halls.

I felt safer doing my route in the morning because at that time the halls were always jammed with kids; at lunch, however, it was far riskier because the halls were nearly deserted. Not even the danger of being caught, however, could deter my desire.

One day, though, a sixth-grade teacher spotted me entering the cafeteria late. "What are you doing out here? You're supposed to come to lunch when everyone else does. If I see you out here again you'll go to the office."

I was so embarrassed my face burned. I was convinced that the whole school was watching me, ready to mock me in unison. After that humiliation I went on my bus route only in the mornings.

They stopped me from going on my bus route in the afternoons, but they couldn't interfere with my number-one rule: No matter what, I made sure I was the last person to get on my bus every day so they all had to wait for me before they could go home. In this way I felt that I had control over the entire school.

Megan got angry with me because I made the other kids wait, but her anger was of no importance to me because of the desire that filled me—my rule must be followed!

Ron had left teaching and was now the public relations director for the city schools, a demanding and stress-filled job. He was the liaison between the Board of Education and the public, attending all the board meetings and dealing with the TV and radio stations and the newspaper. He was attempting to reverse the negative image of the city schools, encouraging the news media to focus on the many achievements of the students rather than the isolated but much more sensational and therefore "newsworthy" negative side. But as far as the press was concerned, one kid caught carrying a knife to school was worth a thousand science-fair winners.

Our evenings at home were never long enough. We wanted to hear about Megan's school day, her adventures with her horse, Quicksilver. I always had piles of papers to grade from my reading classes with 150 students a day, lesson plans to create for the following day. And every night—*every* night—we talked to Sean. We went over and over the same ground with him, trying to think of new examples, fresh ways of stating the same truth: If you do *this*, you cause *that*. We had replaced most of the violence with words, taking Sean to his room when his disruptive behavior began in earnest and talking to him, sometimes for an hour, more often for two. Most nights it was Ron who sat with Sean, trying to get him to see what his behavior was doing to us all. He was patient, refusing to get angry with his son because he knew it never worked. But patience is a struggle and it took its toll.

Once, when we were alone together, Ron said, "I hate what he does to you and Megan—in some ways he's worse than ever, and he's fourteen years old! I can't get over the lurking suspicion that he behaves this way on purpose, that he wants us to live in hell. I know that's crazy, but sometimes I look at him and he seems so damn *knowing!*"

"Yes, he sure does. As if he knows exactly what he's doing and he enjoys it. But it's not like that."

"Of course I know that. I've finally given up on the idea that shaking him will connect the wires in his head that don't quite meet. I mean it's really nuts to think that, but for years that's how I felt!"

"Me too."

"And now," Ron went on, "I think that if we just keep hammering away at him with cause and effect he'll get it— maybe it'll be the ten-thousandth time we have the same conversation, but eventually it will happen and he'll see it. We can't just give up."

"I know."

One night, though, the patience ran out.

———

I will never forget the spring when I was fourteen. It was then that I experienced the most terrifying thing that ever happened to me—my dad stopped speaking to me for eight straight days.

I don't even remember the behavior that caused it—I think it may have been an accumulation of things. Whatever the reason, it seemed minor to me, certainly no worse than any of the other things I did that got me yelled at. So what the hell had I done?

It had been a bad week. I was being yelled at for every god-damned thing under the sun. My established rules were not being followed the way they should have been—Megan was coming downstairs in the mornings before me, my family refused to sit in the chairs I assigned them, and my bus was one of the first to arrive at school every afternoon. Usually I was furious at my school bus and would get home in a really rotten mood. As a result of my bad mood I'd do something, and right away Mom would get mad at me. I'd be home ten minutes and already we'd be fighting! I knew that my family, as well as the rest of the world, was completely against me.

All week at school the kids tormented me mercilessly; then, when he got home, Dad would be mad at me as well. I guess he had just heard too much arguing and teasing. We were all at home one evening when I must have done one too many things wrong. Until this time I had felt fairly safe with him because he rarely got fed up with me. Mom, on the other hand, got mad at me for almost everything. This time, though, Dad said to me, "You've been angry with me for fourteen years—now I'm going to be angry with you for the next fourteen years! I'm not talking to you anymore!" My feelings of security evaporated instantly.

The effect of his words grew inside me like a tumor. I was so shaken that I had no way to rationalize what he meant, nor could I figure out what I had done to cause such a reaction from him so that I could avoid doing it again. I took what he said literally. I thought, "Sean, you better get used to it, because he's not going to say one sentence to you until you turn twenty-eight!"

I wanted to run away, perhaps live on the streets. There was, though, a small part of me that was still hopeful—so many times both my parents had been enraged with me, yet no matter how mad they got, they always got over it. If I did something praiseworthy, then the vile stuff would certainly be washed away. So, I thought, why should this time be any different? However, I had badly misjudged the situation.

Dad spent the whole night not saying one word to me. The next morning he left for work before I was up. Since I was bracing for the next decade-and-a-half of silence, I deeply hoped he would have a great day at work and come home in a sparkling mood, and that everything would be forgotten.

When I got home from school my fear was rekindled. All day I had been thinking, "Does he really think I've been angry with him for fourteen years? But why?" I felt enormously tense when I heard the crunching of tires on our driveway. I watched from my bedroom window as Dad approached the house. I decided to stay in my own room a little while longer, then I would just walk down the stairs and greet him with the best mood I could muster.

Fifteen minutes later I got the strength to go downstairs. "Hi, Dad!"

"Sean, I'm not talking to you." I retreated upstairs feeling about two inches tall and burst into tears. My worst fears had been confirmed. Not only had he not gotten over it, he was going to deny his own son's existence for fourteen years! I wanted to end my life— if I hadn't been so afraid of pain, I might have taken a sharp knife from the kitchen and plunged it into my chest!

Several days passed and nothing changed. Dad would come home and greet Mom and Meg, ignoring me. In the meantime I tried my best to be helpful in any way I could. I mowed the lawn, dried the dishes—anything to win Dad back. After three days of living in a house with a man who was killing me emotionally, I decided to run away. But where could I go? I had no friends, no money. So I decided instead to keep trying to help around the house, hoping that in time, Dad's heart would thaw and he would talk to me again. Each time I did something good I hoped it would take a chip out of Dad's arrogance. Eight days passed with no change.

One afternoon I was mowing the lawn when Dad approached me. "Sean, I'm very sorry for not talking to you. I see how much you've been helping around the house. Your mother has told me how you've been helping her as well." It was over at last! *At first his words confused me, but then I was so relieved that I couldn't get myself to say anything. We hugged each other and tears welled up in my eyes. I apologized for what I'd done and swore I'd do my damnedest to stay out of trouble. I still felt that I could not control my behavior or my impulses, but I swore to myself that I would try.*

Sometimes during those eight days the fear I had was so great that I felt sick. I had tried to stop myself from doing those things for which I always got yelled at—teasing the dogs and Megan, and asking my repetitious questions. I thought that if Dad was so angry with me that he could refuse to speak to me altogether, then he was capable of doing anything he wanted to me if I crossed him. One of the worst things was having to go to bed at night without his saying goodnight to me. He was taller than I was and he was faster and stronger; these things, combined with his anger, scared the hell out of me. What was to stop him from coming into my room in the middle of the night and, in a fit of rage, killing me? If I provoked him again, maybe by teasing Meg one too many times, he might actually resort to murder!

When he began speaking to me again, my fear was replaced with relief. But I also had a new awareness—I knew I had to change my behavior somehow, no matter how hard it would be. What really upset me was that I didn't know how I could stop myself from doing the things everyone disliked; if I did stop, how long could I keep it up? After all, my behavior controlled me, not the other way around.

Megan and I pleaded with Ron to stop the war with Sean, but we were unable to change his mind. He was relentless.

"I've had it. I've reached the end of the road with him— nothing we do makes any difference. There has to be something that will get through to him! I feel like the worst father in the world right now, but I don't know what the hell to do—I want to *save* him. The only thing that might work is something this extreme! Nothing else has!"

As much as I disagreed with the method, it was obvious that Sean was affected, that for the first time he understood that his behavior had caused his father to stop talking to him. He was a different child that week, offering to help around the house, fighting to control his compulsiveness.

When it was finally over he came to me. "Mom, I think Dad loves me again." I held him and he held me back.

Sean entered high school—a fifteen-year-old ninth grader in a regular public school. He was one of more than 1,600 white, middle-class kids in a building with vast corridors, sophisticated science, math, and language labs, and an ocean of strange faces. We were terrified for him, yet he seemed relieved.

I still remembered the anxiety I had felt when I went to high school—a place much smaller and cozier than the huge building Sean would have to adjust to. However, he seemed to be doing just that. He was most frightened of his English class, where he was required to write themes, something he said he simply could not do. His grades, though, continued to be above average.

The subject that was more difficult for him than any he had yet encountered was wood shop. We didn't realize the severity of his problem until well after the class was over. When his compulsive behavior at home got worse, we knew there was something wrong, but for a long time we didn't know what it was. As always, he evaded our questions and volunteered nothing, never asking for help.

One day he said he had to go to school the following morning, a Saturday. Why on a weekend?

"Oh, some of us are going to do a little extra work on our projects in shop class."

"What is the project?"

"It's like a little drawer thing."

"Is it for extra credit, you mean?"

"I guess so."

He was behind everyone else in his class, one of the neighbor boys told us. Ron, skilled at carpentry, offered help. "Can you bring your project home and we'll work on it together?"

"No."

"Then can I explain something you're having a problem with?"

"It will be fine. I can do it."

At the end of the term Megan brought home her report card. Sean didn't.

"Where is yours?" I asked.

"I didn't get one."

"Why not?"

"I don't know. No one in my class got one."

I called the school. Everyone had, of course, received grade cards.

"Sean, where is it?"

"I didn't get one."

"But you did. I know that. Did you lose it, or did you get low grades? Because if that's it, you know it's okay with us. We know you're working hard and that's all that's important."

Silence. "Sean, will you show it to me, please?"

"I didn't get one."

I was in ninth grade. Though it was rather scary at first, it also gave me a small sense of renewal, even a feeling of relief and security. I was at a brand-new school with many more kids, and I stood less of a chance of seeing the awful kids who had teased me at the other school. I felt as if I were beginning the year with a partially clean slate. I was hopeful.

I had to take a class in wood shop. Had I known how the experience in this class would turn out, I probably would have packed my bags and boarded a bus to Point Barrow, Alaska! The teacher, Mr. Hall, was an older man who demanded that all the students conform and, I thought, he wouldn't hesitate to blow a person's head off with a rifle if anyone defied him. The very first day he screamed at a kid who wasn't listening to him—the first day, for God's sake! What would happen to me if he caught me rubbing my eyes during one of his lectures? I was completely intimidated by him.

I had never made anything out of wood before, and with each passing day, as he explained the use of all the tools, my confidence slowly ebbed away.

Not until the middle of the semester were we given our assignments. We were to build a small square box and a drawer to fit into it. He warned us that an incomplete project would automatically mean an F. That comment sent a wave of panic through me.

True to my expectations, as the weeks progressed, I got farther and farther behind. The horrible thought of my first-ever F was in my mind at all times. Some of the other kids were actually sympathetic and tried to help me.

I went into the shop every Saturday—Mr. Hall had told us that if we were having trouble and needed more time, he would open the shop for us. I knew my having to be there meant only one thing—I was way behind on my work and didn't know what the hell I was doing! The other students seemed to find the assignment very easy, and my feelings of frustration and failure increased. I was afraid to ask Mr. Hall for help because I was sure he would think I hadn't been listening to him. So I plugged on.

I could see that I'd never be able to complete my project before the end of the semester. I kept thinking, "How will I ever be able to face anyone if I get an F? Meg is on the Honor Roll, getting all A's and B's, and here I am getting a goddamned F!"

The end of the semester approached. One day, Mr. Hall took me aside. He explained to me that he was not going to fail me after all even though I was only half-finished with the box.

"Sean, I'm going to give you credit for trying—I can see how hard you've worked by coming in every Saturday morning."

"What grade will you give me, then?"

"You'll be getting a D," he said.

At this news I felt several things at once. There was a twinge of relief, yet I was hugely disappointed as well—I still felt like a failure since everyone else had finished their project. I went home with my half-finished box, dejected.

I put the box in my room. It didn't seem to have any use as far as I could see. Besides, the letter grade said it all: This project received a D; therefore, it is a below-average piece of work. After awhile the box began to feel like an insult sitting there. I wanted to get rid of it.

One day Mom yelled at me for the millionth time, and I responded with immense anger. Our argument escalated to the point where I grabbed the box, ran out the back door to the woods behind our house, and, in a blind rage, hit myself on the side of the head with the box, time after time. I didn't black out but I felt dizzy. With my anger still raging, I took the drawer out and threw it against a tree with all my might! I stomped on the box until there was nothing left of it but a shapeless pile of wooden pieces; then I threw the whole thing into the woods.

Since the first weeks of school I had chosen to spend much of my time in the principal's office. It was clear that I wasn't going to make any *friends my own age, and at least in the office the adults didn't tease and humiliate me; I felt far more comfortable with them. Since my own father had been a teacher in this high school and knew most of the staff, I felt that I, too, could befriend the teachers and administrators. Screw the students! I thought. I don't need them!*

One of the guidance counselors, Mrs. Bennett, was especially nice to me and introduced me to the other people in the office. Mrs. Bennett was very appealing, and in no time at all I was in love with her. It wasn't that she had any striking physical features, and the age difference between us was quite wide, but she was interested in me as a person. As had been the case two years earlier with my science teacher, I had to keep my feelings for Mrs. Bennett a secret. If anybody were to find out, I'd be done for!

I visited Mrs. Bennett more and more often as the year went on. I couldn't wait for lunch period because instead of going to the cafeteria, I went to the office, where I hoped to find her door open. Often I spent the entire lunch period with her. I didn't care about not eating lunch if it meant I could have her all to myself.

I made it clear to Mrs. Bennett how I felt about her. I did this by giving her cards on special occasions—Thanksgiving, Christmas, St. Patrick's Day, etc. I gave her intimate cards coated with syrupy language. The first four times she thanked me for the card and for my thoughtfulness; my feelings were reinforced!

My infatuation with her became so fierce that she occupied nearly all my thoughts. As a result I dreaded weekends and holidays because we would be separated from each other. The end came in April.

I carefully selected a card to give her for Easter. It was laden with sentiment, and I wrote on it as well, expressing how I felt so she would know I was deeply in love. I gave her the card.

I was sitting in study hall when the teacher handed me a pink

summons slip saying I was to see Mrs. Bennett right away. Fright-
ened, I left the room as inconspicuously as possible.

When I got to her room Mrs. Bennett was there and so was the
school psychologist. "Close the door, Sean," Mrs. Bennett said.

I did, and sat down across from the two of them. "Sean, I want to
talk to you about this card you gave me." I sat there trembling as the
room began closing in on me. The floor under my feet would open
and I'd fall through it into a bottomless pit.

"I must tell you that I am not your sweetheart. I am your friend."

"Sean, you have a crush on Mrs. Bennett," the psychologist said.
"Your feelings, though, cannot be returned by her."

Mrs. Bennett explained that she had a husband who felt toward
her the same way I said I felt and that it would be unnatural for her to
love me the way she loved him.

"I'm going to get suspended then, huh?" I asked. I felt like a
defendant who had just been convicted of double homicide.

"No, no, no. You won't be suspended. It's just that I can't be your
sweetheart—you need to find someone your own age to feel that way
about."

I knew she was a woman at least three times my age and that she
had a husband. But I didn't know what these facts meant and had no
idea why I shouldn't be in love with her or she with me. How
shocking it was for her to point out where I had gone awry! And now
I had no real friend again.

Sean and I had incessant verbal battles. I knew better than to
get trapped in one, that it would only lead to anger and frustration for us both, yet I'd open my mouth and say precisely what I
knew I shouldn't say.

He couldn't stand to take any instructions from me because he heard them as criticism:

"Sean, put your dishes in the sink."

"I was just on my way to do that."

"No, you were on your way out the door."

"I was going to do it first, then go outside."

"But you were already out the door."

"I was only checking the temperature."

"Why can't you just say, 'Okay'?"

"Because Sean hates to be corrected. Sean is an asshole!"

"Look, I wasn't correcting you—I just asked you to put your dishes in the sink the way the rest of us do. Anyhow, *all* parents correct their kids—that's how they learn. It doesn't mean you're bad!"

But to him, it did.

He wanted to use the longest words he could find to impress people. For a long time he got stuck on chemical compounds and inserted several of them into every conversation. "Carbamylachloride" and "fluorophosphate" would pop up when you least expected them.

I became aware that people used language to communicate with one another, but I didn't know how this was done. I got the idea that big words were a sign of intelligence. So, to make myself smarter, I decided to read the Random House Dictionary. *It was the biggest one we had.*

That day, after school, I started reading with the first definition. Every day I read as much as I could, concentrating as hard as possible. Nearly eight weeks later I finished the dictionary. I felt a sense of power, and I was eager to have people hear me use these words! I didn't know how to use them in context, I realized years later. But when I was fifteen I thought I could just substitute a big word for a small one and everyone would say, "Boy, is he smart!"

When my plan failed I was baffled and hurt. At first I was angry with everyone, but then I knew what it really meant: I still didn't have a clue as to how people talked to one another. Not for the first time, I felt like an alien from outer space—I had no more idea how to communicate with people than a creature from another planet.

"Sean, that's just not the way kids talk!" I'd say after hearing him hold forth with a baffled neighbor boy. "Listen to them—they don't use those kinds of words. You don't have to prove anything to other kids, just be natural! Don't try to impress them with big words, it makes them think you're showing off."

I introduced him to a friend we ran into in a parking lot. Sean said to him, "My, what pleasant nocturnal air we are encountering this evening. It puts me in a very ebullient mood. I'm gratified to meet you."

My friend looked from Sean to me with a smile. Then he laughed, hoping it was safe to do so. I wanted to explain that my fifteen-year-old son had learned English in the Kweichow Province of China.

"Why did he laugh?" Seán said angrily as we got into the car.

"It was your choice of words, Sean. He thought you were *trying* to be funny—no one talks that way. When you say things like that to people, they don't know what you're doing. See, no one uses long words like that when they're talking to each other."

"Sometimes you and Dad use long words."
"But not if there's a simple way of saying something."
"Then what are long words for? Why are the goddamn things in the goddamn dictionary?"

Everything set him apart from the other kids, when all he wanted was to be accepted. He gave no thought to his appearance, refusing *ever* to look at himself in a mirror. He still washed only the front of his hair and never combed it, he put on clothes with stains or tears. Desperate for friends, longing to look "normal," he'd come home from school on the days he had gym class with his shirt buttoned haphazardly, the collar stuck inside the neck, his pants half-zipped, tufts of hair sticking up on his head in clumps.

"Honey, look—if you want to make friends then you have to pay attention to how you look."

"I look fine."

"No, sometimes you don't. You're a very good-looking boy, but you have to look in the mirror to check on how you look to other people. We all do that."

"They should like me because I'm a nice person."

"Sure, but first they have to get to know you, and kids notice the way you look—so do adults!"

"But they have no right to!"

Right.

Every time I caught sight of myself in the mirror, I was flooded with shame and embarrassment. I felt I was such a terrible person that I could not look at myself.

This is what I knew—all the other kids at Boardman High School got along perfectly with their families. I knew that. No one else got yelled at except me. So when Mom or Dad yelled at me I pictured the other kids watching me and laughing; they were thinking, "What an awful person he is—getting yelled at by his own parents!" These pictures I got were more than images—it was as if the kids were really there.

So seeing myself in the mirror—even a glance—opened the flood-gates of humiliation. If I was forced to look, I made sure my eyes were over my head or to one side. I couldn't face myself and all that negativity.

With clothes it was the same thing—I knew everybody in the world knew how to get dressed without instructions, so why did I have to be corrected? What I did was never right, never good enough. I never once thought about clothes that went together; I had no sense of that. I had no idea how you could tell if a shirt was buttoned wrong, I didn't realize that the flaps at the bottom had to be the same length. So how the hell could Mom tell? It amazed me that she could just look at me and say, "Your shirt is buttoned wrong." How did she know?

I had a lot of trouble fastening buttons through the holes and tying shoes. Many times I ripped the buttons off my shirts and broke my laces because I was so furious with the damn things when they refused to work. I knew my problems with clothes were another thing that set me apart from the other kids.

Mom told me I should try to look at myself and dress carefully. That made me angry and irritated, so I shut out her voice. I simply would not look in the mirror, no matter what!

Nearly every time I talked with Sean I thought—Why not shut up and let him say and do whatever he wants? But his words were as compulsive as his actions, and I was determined to break through them. If I kept trying, I figured, he would eventually understand me; the problem was, if he was incapable of that understanding, I was torturing him.

Things got worse at school. Several of the teachers reported that Sean walked through the halls looking straight ahead and speaking to no one; even when they spoke to him by name, he ignored them. He was the kid to pick on—he was weird, retarded, out of it. There were tormentors in every class; although it was actually only two or three kids, it felt to Sean as if those kids represented all the others.

One morning we awoke to find that our newly painted house had been pelted with eggs, the yard and trees littered with garbage. The high school principal suspected Joey, the most visible of Sean's persecutors, and when confronted, Joey confessed. The principal sent him to our home to clean up the damage (though the whole front of the house had to be repainted) and to apologize to us.

He was a good-looking boy with a kind face. I was shocked. Ron and I sat down with him in the living room and told him about Sean, what it was like to be Sean. He listened intently.

"So you see," I said, "everything he does is a struggle for him—everything the rest of us do so easily without even thinking. And he's the perfect kid to pick on—he sure doesn't act like anybody else, and he even looks different. He can't even figure out how to defend himself! More than anything he wants to be like all the other kids, but he knows he's different—he just doesn't know why. But I can tell you that he's so hurt by what you and the other kids do to him at school that he almost can't go there anymore."

"But I—we—didn't really mean to hurt him. I mean, he acts

like it doesn't even matter, like he doesn't notice us. He won't react to what we do or say. We just meant it to be funny, kind of, when we tease him . . . that sounds stupid."

"I understand what you mean," Ron said. "You thought he's just not like you and your friends. But look at his eyes when you call him names and imagine what it would feel like if you had a gang of kids making fun of you, calling you retarded, shooting paper clips at you. That's exactly how he feels—he's on the outside, he feels he doesn't fit in anywhere, and it hurts him so much that he has to pretend it isn't happening. That's why he doesn't react."

Joey asked if he could see Sean before he left. We called him in from the backyard. Joey said, "Look . . . I just want to tell you I'm sorry. I've been a bastard to you and I won't be one anymore. I—uh, I've been real dumb."

Sean took the hand he held out and shook it. "That's okay."

Joey kept his word. Neither he nor any of his friends was cruel to Sean again.

———

At this time in my life I found a new interest—astronomy. This science was titillating because it was the next best thing to a real escape—an exit from the jackass kids at my high school. Besides, just as with the TV call letters with which I was still fascinated, this was knowledge I perceived to be esoteric. Once again I established power. Astronomy filled part of my void of loneliness as well. I could deal with phenomena that were "out there," and it helped me get away from my present situation.

I loved studying the various planets because that made it much easier to imagine being elsewhere. I basked in the soothing comfort of my own fantasies. Sometimes I would stare at photographs of Mars;

then I would blast off and arrive on the planet itself, with its barren landscape and desolate craters. From Mars I could look down on Earth, so far away. Ohio was down there somewhere, but too far away to hurt me. This was a world I had to myself, and I felt free, rejuvenated. At times like this my pain and insecurities would slowly evaporate until I began to feel something approaching normal. Then, of course, Mom would have to call and make me come downstairs.

When I reached tenth grade there was a change in my attitude. I still had no ability to relate to my fellow students, but now I felt I had put my situation with the teachers and administrators into perspective—I no longer wanted to be friends with them. My feelings had swung to the other extreme, in fact; I wanted nothing whatever to do with any of them. I did everything I could to avoid them, including, of course, Mrs. Bennett. In some way I knew that I was even more alienated from everyone than I had been the year before, but that's just how it was and had to be. I was erasing the school's figures from my life—the students and the adults. I did this by inventing a game—it was a baseball game and I was the pitcher.

It was my way of getting even with the adults who had not conformed to my rules and expectations. I made a mental list of those I felt had betrayed me. This is how I set it up: Each school month was one inning; if I succeeded in going the entire year without certain people seeing me, then I would have pitched a no-hitter! It worked out perfectly—there were nine months in the school year! Next, I assigned each person a particular value: If Mr. Lesser saw me and said hello, it was only a single, but if Mrs. Bennett saw me and spoke to me, then I'd given up a home run. The more I needed to avoid the person, the higher their value.

The first week of my sophomore year I spoke to a total of no one. I had begun pretending there was no one in the school but me. My *feelings about Mrs. Bennett from the previous spring—when she told me she couldn't love me—turned into a new emotion: an overwhelming desire to get even! She was at the epicenter of my fury. I vowed that by the end of this year, everyone who had hurt me in any way would be punished. My baseball game was my way of making these people pay for what they had done.*

There was one big problem with my game—the people I was determined to avoid were the very ones I was drawn to. The thing was, if I was successful in avoiding them, then how would they know how furious I was with them? So, part of me hoped that I would run into them even as I tried not to.

Most of the time I would simply turn and face the opposite direction when someone on my list approached. However, if I was in a negative mood and felt like letting out some of my bottled-up anger, I would shun them.

It was almost six months before I saw Mrs. Bennett. One day I was sitting on my bench adjacent to but out of sight of the cafeteria. Mrs. Bennett came down the hall toward the teachers' lounge. As usual during lunch, I had brought my astronomy book and was studying some aspect of the planets while everyone else was eating. Now, as Mrs. Bennett approached, I pulled several star charts from my book and held them up, pretending to be engrossed in the positions of the constellations. I didn't look at her as she came up to me.

"Hi, Sean."

No reply from me; no contact.

"Sean—how are you?"

I continued staring at the charts as if I hadn't heard her. She stood there a moment longer, then gave up and disappeared into the lounge. I put down my star charts, feeling quite satisfied. Partial revenge had been obtained!

The way I dealt with the hundreds of other students was to look down at the floor as I trudged through the halls. I convinced myself that no one was there but me, that I was completely alone in the school.

I applied this rule of mine to my sister, Megan, also. My sister was a person I had never understood well, and I spent much of my life feeling jealous of her. Those feelings were planted early on. Even when she was a little child, everything had been easy for her. It made me insanely furious that I was always being yelled at for doing what I loved, yet Megan could do whatever she wanted and she was always accepted! She got along with everyone; I got along with no one. During our school years, no matter how good my grades were, hers were always better. There were many, many times when I despised her.

On the other hand, Megan and I had our own special bond. Sometimes we did things that no one else could comprehend, and we even had our own language in a way. Besides, I could display power over her by inventing a game with rules for her to follow, then break those same rules myself. That helped me get back at her for making me feel inferior to her.

As we got older I saw Meg's personality changing—I had always been able to control her reactions to me; I could make her angry exactly when I wanted to. But now she got furious with me when I didn't expect it, and her anger was more intense. Since Meg was the only person I ever had good times with, I was afraid she'd decide she didn't want to have anything more to do with me. I realized she was the only friend I had! So at home I was frightened of her, not knowing how to control her anymore.

At school I simply tried to avoid my sister. Because I felt inferior to her my rules were that much more important. Since she made me feel inadequate, I just pretended she didn't exist. The more I denied her, the more power I had over her.

Then, in January 1978, I got some totally unexpected and deeply shocking news. One morning Dad called me down to the living room to talk to me. "Sean, I want to tell you something important. I've decided to take the job in California, and we'll be moving to Los Angeles very soon."

"What!?" At first I thought he was kidding. "Do you mean we're moving away?"

"Yes. But I want you to tell me how you feel about this."

I knew Dad had been offered a job in California and that my parents had been discussing it, but for the first time the seriousness of the whole thing hit me and tears entered my eyes. Trying my best not to cry, I stated my case and defended my position—my opposition to the move. I defended my school, our neighbors, the town we lived in. I put the school I hated in another context by saying that things would get better for me there if we chose to stay. But it was no use.

Dad tried to persuade me that things would improve for me once I adjusted to a new life in California, but I couldn't stand the thought of moving away from the only place I had ever known. I didn't sleep for several nights after our talk. My future was in jeopardy!

Because the first sixteen years of my life had been so awful, one might think that I would have loved the idea of moving away. After all, it was a way out of my very painful circumstances. But I hated change, all change! I loved repetition, and the more my environment stayed the same, the less threatened I felt. The reason I hated listening to pop stations on the radio, for example, was that they kept changing the songs they played; I couldn't tolerate it when a new building was erected where there hadn't been one before, nor could I take it when one was torn down. I hated it when people did things out of order, when they sat in chairs that were not theirs, when they said things they were not supposed to say.

So what could disrupt my life more than a move to California? It *was a place I had never even seen! My structure was being violated in every possible way. I still bitterly resented that I had been prevented from going to my school for a full year when I was in fourth and fifth grades, and now they were doing it again!!* I wanted events to follow established, predictable patterns!

As some time passed, though, I allowed myself to think that such a move might offer certain benefits. I thought, "Maybe I will be happier there, who the hell knows?" There were two things I could look forward to—an escape from winter (I had a rule that there was to be no snow) and new TV and radio station call letters to watch and listen to.

When the day came for our move to Los Angeles, I said good-bye to no one. I was there one day and gone the next, 2,500 miles away! I wanted to be cleansed of the poisonous effects of contact with the other students. I wanted them to find out on their own that I was no longer theirs to torment. By the time they knew, I would be an entire length of a country away from them.

This is how I felt: I was taking the biggest risk of my whole life by forfeiting all the security I had built up in sixteen years. My own future was spinning out of control.

I n March 1978 Ron and I, wearing fake fur coats, stood with Megan and Sean on the sidewalk at LAX. Piled around us was a mountain of suitcases and carryalls. Our two groggy dogs, both tranquilized in sky-kennels, howled disconsolately. It was pouring for the sixth straight day, and the ground had become a mire; houses in Malibu were following tradition and sliding into the sea; endless traffic crawled along the freeways, which were littered with overheated cars, their hoods raised.

We were moving to California—land of sunshine. I had resigned from teaching, Ron from his job as Director of Community Relations of the Youngstown Public Schools. We had sold our house, two cars, Megan's horse. We had packed everything we owned and sent it ahead of us in a moving van. We were buying a house in Los Angeles, a place our children had never seen, and we were both going into the entertainment business, I to write lyrics, Ron to comanage Maureen McGovern, the singer from our hometown with whom we had been close friends for years. Now, instead of giving advice from the periphery of her life, the three of us would work together on her career.

The course of our lives in Ohio had become numbingly predictable—teaching became harder every year as the students' concentration spans grew shorter, in direct proportion, I believed, to the amount of television they watched. It became

208

more difficult for us teachers to reach their individuality, their unique talents and points of view. The teachers I worked with, in their thirties and younger, were already talking about retirement. Ron's job had run itself out when the man for whom he had worked, the first black school superintendent in Ohio, took a university position, and it appeared that the school system was about to slide backward from the progress toward racial equality that had been made under his leadership.

The path of our lives in Ohio was clear; we could see what the future would hold. All my life I had hated repetition, so I taught each of my six reading classes differently, varied the details of my life as much as I could. But no matter what I did, a voice somewhere in my head whispered, "If I can see my future spun out before my eyes, why live it?" So we changed lives.

Of course, much of the desire for such a drastic upheaval was a result of our continuing failure with our son. I couldn't stand the idea of staying in the trough of our lives, simply watching Sean grow older. I knew how he dreaded even the smallest change, that only predictability made him feel secure. But security hadn't helped him. Changing everything he knew would have a major effect on him, we thought. But would he progress or retreat inside himself, maybe for good? We felt we had to take the chance.

Fortuitously, Megan's two closest friends were moving away from Ohio as well, so it was much less painful for her to make the change.

———

About three hours into the flight from Pittsburgh to Los Angeles, I looked down and saw that the ground was no longer covered with snow. The winter in Ohio had been unusually harsh and cruel, and I had hated it—the constantly gray and overcast skies had made me feel hopeless and dead inside. Snow had always been my enemy, forcing me to spend my time trapped in the house with my mother. Now I felt a thrill of excitement; we were leaving winter behind forever! I was out of its clutches at last!

Then immediately my elation disappeared, replaced by a sickening terror and dread. What was going to happen to me? I thought about the night before, our last night in Ohio, when I had tried to go to sleep but had been so overcome with fear that I'd vomited. Now that feeling was back.

As we left the plane I felt my first California earthquake. It was inside my own stomach and legs. Even as I knew I was going to be sick, I noticed that the temperature in LA was 62 degrees, and I almost smiled to think that back in Ohio it had been close to 0.

Why were we suddenly in Los Angeles? All I knew was that my parents were going to work with a friend of theirs, Maureen McGovern, but I had no idea what they planned to do. As we drove to the San Fernando Valley, where they told me we would live, I wanted to shout, "Take me home! I want to go back to Ohio!" But I didn't say anything to anyone because I knew it would do no good.

They told me we were going to buy a new house, that I would like it and have my own room as I had before. But the thing was, the house wasn't ready yet, and we had to move into a rented house temporarily. I wasn't even going to get a real home!

I was in California for the first time, a new state and one I had always wanted to visit, and I was seeing mountains for the first time as well; I got no pleasure from any of it. I couldn't focus on anything because my future and my destiny were in jeopardy, in the hands of other people. I felt as if I had been kidnapped, except that I knew my abductors, and no amount of money would get me back to my own life in Ohio. I was lost and felt abandoned.

During our first week in LA Megan and I didn't go to school. I sat and stared out the window at the mountains. I knew that Ohio lay somewhere far, far beyond those mountains and that maybe if I climbed to the top, I could see my home from there. I knew that one day soon I would try it and if, when I reached the top, I was unable to see Ohio, I would throw myself off the mountainside. My mind was a vast expanse and my stomach a series of intertwined knots.

For the first few days I refused to react to anything; I was somewhere else, somewhere inside my head. Then, in the middle of the week, I said to Mom just as she was waking up, "I'm not going to go to school here. That's my decision."

"Sean, you'll like the school. Remember how nice the principal was when you met him?" she said. (My parents had taken me to see the school so I'd know what I was in for.) I didn't care; I wasn't going. The school was wrong. It in no way resembled my "real" school—the room numbers were in the wrong order and there were several separate one-story buildings. School had to be only one building with three floors.

"I just said I'm not going!"

"Come on, we've been through this so many times—don't start it again!" Mom said angrily.

I stalked out of the bedroom. At that moment I realized that the incessant fighting between Mom and me would continue even though we had moved 2,500 miles away. Once I recovered from the shock of moving, I now saw, the flames of hell would be rekindled; I would lose control of my behavior again and continue on a downward spiral. My nightmare would begin all over again.

I did go to school after all. The place was a haphazard array of buildings that made no sense, and I felt smaller and more insignificant than ever. I felt that I was inside a dream and not really there at all. After a few days I began to notice the other students, although I never looked into their eyes—I knew better than to do that. There were many black kids and a lot of others who spoke Spanish. I couldn't figure out why they would travel all the way from Spain to go to school there. I didn't know at the time that people from many other countries spoke Spanish. There were a lot of other foreign students too, but I had no idea what nationalities they were. I couldn't make sense of anything I saw.

After a few weeks I was hit with a realization: No one here seemed to notice me or to see anything odd about me. I started to relax a little bit. Then a new thought struck me and fear filled me again: Someone in my old school would find out where I was, would know someone in this new school, and would describe me to him. I was sure of it. Someone here was looking for me. No matter how hard I tried to fit in and stay undercover, eventually my "behavior" would surface and I'd be found. The teasing and tormenting would start all over. They would all know.

I tried to live in a vacuum. I went through school the same way I had in Ohio, pretending no one else was there. One day I had to use a restroom between classes, and I went into one I'd never seen before. It was a dark, windowless place and every wall was covered with graffiti. The writing shocked and scared me because it was so violent and obscene. I was used to seeing things like "Tom Loves Laurie" on the walls.

Five Chicano kids were clustered against one wall, smoking, and I pretended not to see them. I didn't want them to know I had noticed the graffiti either. As I tried to leave the restroom, one of the group, a short, stocky boy, moved in front of me and blocked the door. He glared at me.

"Where the fuck you think you're going, man?"

"I have to go to my next class," I said as gently as possible.

"You ain't going nowhere, man!"

"Come on, let me go. I'll be late."
I thought: So this is the kid, the one who's been watching for me.
The boy was spread-eagled across the doorway. I lunged and tried
to duck under his arm, but he caught me around the neck in a
crunching hold. The other kids surrounded me, laughing and jeering.
I heard the tardy bell ring and suddenly he let go of me. I walked past
him and out of the restroom. I refused to run because I would not call
attention to myself in any way. Behind me someone yelled, "What a
fuckin' pussy!"
For the next few days I watched for him. Several times I did see
him, but he didn't seem to recognize me. I began to believe that he
didn't know who I was and that I had probably been a random
victim. Otherwise he never would have let up on me.

Suddenly we had no set working hours, no schedule except the one we made for ourselves, and no regular paychecks. Every day was different, filled with new people and experiences, unusual events.

The kids were enrolled in ninth and tenth grades in the Los Angeles public school system. Megan, in junior high (because high school in California begins with the tenth grade), found herself doing work that she had done three and four years earlier in Ohio. We were shocked. What about the reputation California had as a leader in the field of education? Megan loved to read, to write, and to be challenged. She was in hell. Ron and I made repeated trips to her school to confer with the teachers: no, she could not be given additional assignments because that took too much of the teachers' time; no, she could not study in the library on her own when she had finished her regular work; no, there was no accelerated class she could transfer to (besides, she was already *in* advanced English and history, a fact she was unaware of); and no, they would not give her a placement test to determine whether she qualified to move on to tenth grade.

During the third conference we'd requested with all of Megan's teachers, her math teacher finally said. "Oh come on, let's face it, most of these kids are Mexicans—they don't care about education, and their families don't give a damn either, so we have to gear our classes to the slowest kids so we can pass them. It's like trying to teach animals in trees!" I looked at the other three teachers, and they stared back expressionless. I felt hot with anger. Ron spoke first: "You people should never be allowed to teach. They should keep you away from those children!" His face was red, the tendons in his neck stood out like ropes.

"It's really too bad," the history teacher added, as if Ron hadn't spoken. "Normally she would be allowed to go to another school with more accelerated classes, but because she's one of a 13 percent minority of white kids, she has to stay here."

The elements of the school system that made our daughter frustrated and miserable seemed to have a different effect on our son. Sean said his high school classes were easy, that he wasn't afraid of the work anymore. He, too, had covered most of the material in Ohio. But the most profound difference was the kids he went to school with—an international mix of every color, nationality, and religion. There was no single standard of behavior or of dress. There was no "look." About a month after he started school in California, Sean came home one afternoon and said, "There are more than 2,000 kids at my school and not one of them knows anything about Sean Barron!"

214

I didn't know anybody my own age. *I looked at all the other students as a big group who were all alike, in spite of their different colors and races. I, on the other hand, was like no one else. I overheard the kids sitting around talking, and I was baffled by what they talked about. Why was what they said to each other perfectly acceptable but what I said was not?*

I did, though, meet some adults who worked with my parents at the recording studio, and one of these people brought about a major change in my life.

Marcia Day was a woman in her late forties who struck me as charming, brilliant, and extremely powerful. She was also very attractive to me. But most important, she took an immediate and overpowering liking to me. She threw her arms around me as if I were a long-lost member of her family. I needed acceptance desperately, and in Marcia I found it. She listened to what I said and always looked at me as if there was not the least thing wrong with me. Right away I vowed that I would not allow myself to get a crush on her the way I had on Miss Jenkins and Mrs. Bennett back in Ohio. I determined that she and I would become just intimate friends.

She became an obsession. The more I saw her the more I wanted to see her. I wanted her to be my mother instead of the one I had. I wanted to be involved in every aspect of her life, and I decided that she would discuss everything about the music business with me the same way she did with Dad. She had five grown and married daughters plus grandchildren, and she spent a lot of time with them, though I didn't like it when she did. What really incensed me was when she gave her time to other people who were not her relatives.

After her initial flood of affection for me, Marcia began to pull back from our relationship. Sometimes when I saw her at the studio, she didn't even say hello to me! When this happened a bubble of hurt formed inside my chest and spread throughout my whole body. I had to find an empty room to go in so that no one would see how damaged I was.

What had I done? Or had some weird behavior surfaced that I hadn't noticed and made her see that I was not the person she thought I was? All I knew was that I had to get her back or I couldn't survive. I made a decision: I would learn every single thing there was to know about the music business so we would have a common ground. In that way I would make myself more interesting and appealing to her and win her back.

But as soon as I started trying to find out about the music business, I discovered how little I knew. I became consumed with anger. My rule was that I did not ask questions when it was something I should know and wanted to know! So I blocked out the information my parents gave me and refused to listen when they talked about their work, even though it was the information I so desperately needed. I was back to square one.

Marcia paid less and less attention to me. I was getting hurt so often that I had begun to feel numb. I had to stop her from ignoring me! Every day after school when I got to the studio, I longed for her to say hello so that I could ignore her and punish her as she deserved. I carried out my plan very effectively, and I began to feel satisfaction instead of hurt. The only trouble was that she didn't seem to react to what I was doing.

My parents did, though. They sat down with me and explained that I could not behave this way, that I could not ignore Marcia and had to be friendly to her instead. They said I had to understand that she could not spend all her time with me, that she did like me very much but that she had a business to run which took most of her time; that she did not hurt me on purpose.

I thought: So I am having an effect on her after all! If I weren't, she never would have told my parents. It's working! Now I knew I'd chosen the right method to pay her back and I was damned if I was going to stop.

That was the first of probably hundreds of talks my parents had with me about Marcia. I never cared what they said because I knew that what I was doing was getting me her attention, even though it was negative. Certainly nothing I had to say was interesting enough for anyone to listen to!

My junior year began, and now Megan and I were in the same school. I saw that she had no trouble adjusting to the campuslike buildings and no trouble making friends either.

Though I was still going through hell with Marcia, her early feelings for me had given me a bit more confidence somehow. Since she had seen the real person inside me, at least for a while, maybe someone else would too.

I began making a real effort to look into the eyes of other kids at school, something that until now I had been too frightened to do. I knew very well that I had to protect the person inside me who wanted so much to come out; I had to move very carefully.

I was fascinated with a boy in my class named Rob. He was the class comedian and made everyone laugh, but he was never obnoxious or rude. Everyone liked him. I studied him, paying close attention to exactly what he said and did. How could I change and become just like him? I admired him because he never made fun of anybody or laughed at their expense. I wanted so much to get to know him, but I never said a word to him. What if I tried to be funny and he didn't respond? I couldn't risk it!

One day I was outside at lunchtime when I saw Megan talking

with another girl, a tall blonde with striking features. As I watched my sister, I was overcome by a powerful feeling of sorrow and remorse. All the times in Ohio when I had seen her at school and had denied her existence flooded over me. I had to get rid of this horrible feeling. I walked toward her, determined to have a "normal" conversation with her and her friend, something I'd never done in my life. I tried to smile.

They looked at me and Meg smiled. "Sean, this is my friend Dianne."

I said, "How do you do. I'm glad to meet you." Something broke inside me but I don't know what it was. I had never spoken those words before, but it was as though they had been waiting on my lips to come out. Now I had said them and they worked! For just a moment I was separated from my past, and I felt light-headed.

Megan and Dianne went to sit down under a large tree, and I stood where I was. Meg looked back at me. "Sean, come and join us!" I did. Several other kids came over and sat down, and I was introduced to all of them. Everyone chatted about school, but I couldn't really hear them—there was a kind of hum inside me that I later realized was happiness. I was very aware that as they talked, they looked at me, too, that they were including me in their group. I believe I'll never forget that day.

In the following weeks I found that the same group of friends met under that tree every day at lunch. Megan would meet me and take me over to join them. In time I felt brave enough to walk over to them on my own. Sitting under that tree, I had the first relaxed moments of my life. I began to feel safe enough to listen to the other kids, and the amazing thing was that I understood what they were saying! It all made sense to me. I began to make a comment or two to see what would happen. I could tell that they thought I was *okay; that I wasn't weird. I started to talk more. One day I heard myself laugh—it was a new sound coming from me, and I hadn't even meant to do it.*

One day after school Meg said, "We're going to the drama club play tonight. Why don't you come, too?"

I felt a clap of fear. I knew I couldn't do it, that I wasn't ready for anything like this. I'd never know what to say; all I had learned was the basic essentials in dealing with other people.

"Come with us," Megan urged. "You'll have fun."

I thought, the hell with it! I hate this goddamned fear!! Maybe if I go I can get rid of some of it.

I went to the play. I watched what went on on stage, but I didn't really get it. It was a comedy and I didn't know what was funny. But all the kids I ate lunch with were there, and they looked genuinely glad to see me. That night I talked with them more than I ever had before, and I sounded just like them.

We watched Sean for signs of what was going on. He volunteered no information about his new school except that the classes were all pretty easy.

I thought I saw certain changes, then was sure I was wrong; it was the same old behavior in a new place. The people we worked with were kind to him, but he alienated them by demanding more than anyone could possibly give. We couldn't make him see that when someone showed affection for him, he tried to absorb the person completely. He had no sense of perspective. I talked to him over and over about how relationships worked, that there were lines one couldn't cross. He didn't listen.

But in the fall he began to talk about school. Several times he referred to someone as a "friend." His relationship with Megan appeared to be changing. They walked to school together, often stopping on the way home at a place where a friend of Meg's was working. Did it mean anything? And if it did, how long would it last? Megan said he was acting much more normal, that he seemed to be trying hard to make friends. She even described his behavior as "sweet" once or twice. I was grateful that she was so kind to him, that despite her own fragility as a new student, she made room for him. Then one Saturday morning Sean said, "I've asked a girl out tonight. We're going bowling."

When I watched the kids at school I saw that many of them were couples. I wanted a girlfriend, but how the hell did you get one?! The idea of asking a girl out made me sick with anxiety. What was I supposed to say? By now I should know these things. Somehow I had to do it.

I picked Pam, the girl who sat next to me in English class. She was very attractive, with long black hair and dark skin. She was very, very quiet, and when she spoke in class I could barely hear her. Our English teacher was a funny man, and when he said something amusing I developed an exaggerated laugh to attract her attention and convey to her that I was a confident person and understood what was funny.

I talked to Pam as much as possible, and I found out that she was a Sioux Indian. Every day I was determined to work up the courage to ask her out, but the bell rang every time before I could force myself to do it.

One Friday morning I said, "Pam, it's really nice out, isn't it?" Then I did it. "I really like to bowl, do you?"

She said, "I'm not very good at it. I go sometimes with my adopted family."

"Would you like to go tomorrow night?"

"Okay." She gave me her phone number.

I called her the next morning. She said, "When do you want to pick me up?"

"But I can't. I don't have a car." (I didn't want to tell her I couldn't drive, either.)

"Oh. Then do you want my mother to take us?"

"Sure. That's fine."

Pam and her mother picked me up at 7:30 that night, and her mother dropped us at the bowling alley. As soon as we went in my stomach turned to ice. I saw that all the lanes were taken and the place was full of people. I left Pam standing by the door and went over to the manager at the desk to ask for a lane. He said, "You'll have to wait an hour—do you want me to put your name on the waiting list?"

I said no. I was in a panic. I had no idea how to fill up a whole hour; we were there to bowl, and it didn't occur to me that we could sit and talk while we waited or that we could go somewhere else. So I lied to her. "The lane will be ready in a minute."

We stood there. I didn't know what to say. After ten minutes Pam suggested I check to see if there was a lane, so I went to the desk but only pretended to talk to the manager. I went back to Pam and said that all the leagues were running over and there was nothing open.

"Well, maybe I should call my mother then. If we can't bowl."

"Okay," I said. I wanted to creep under a big rock. I was a real fuck-up.

On the way home I didn't say anything, and I was back at my house by 8:00.

When I saw Pam at school on Monday, I couldn't look at her. But after a few days, we began to talk again. Finally, I worked up the nerve to ask her out a second time. In fact, I asked her out several more times, but she never said yes again.

On Christmas Eve we finally moved into our own house—nine months after we should have! Another of my rules had been broken—I had been told that the house would be ready in March—so now I didn't want to live in it at all.

I felt even worse when I walked through the place. "Ready" should have meant exactly that—everything should have been perfectly clean and in order—but the house was dirty, and it needed to be painted. I knew what that meant: Mom would expect me to help her.

Sure enough, we had a brand-new source of arguments for the days to come. She'd say, "Sean, will you help me wash these cupboards?"

I'd respond with, "I'll be right back. I have to do something right now."

"What do you have to do?"

"Just something," I'd say as I left. I deeply resented being expected to help someone who still yelled at me, and besides, I refused to work on a house that was supposed to be ready.

We were buying a house from a family that was building another house nearby, but one construction delay after another put off the transaction. The individual delays were usually a matter of a week or so, but they added up to nine months in all.

Our belongings had been in storage so long that we'd forgotten what we had. We moved in at last on Christmas Eve, and emptying the boxes filled with things we hadn't seen since we left Ohio was like opening Christmas presents.

Ron and I got a tree and put it up. Then we began to work feverishly to do as much as possible to get settled, so that we could have a real Christmas dinner. We worked most of the night, slept a few hours, and started again early Christmas morning. It was starting to look like our home. The turkey was roasting, the bedrooms had been set up, and we had washed everything we needed to have a real holiday dinner. Ron went to take a shower as Megan and I finished unpacking and washing the dishes. We burned all the small boxes and the paper packing materials in our dining room fireplace, adding to the festive air.

Sean carried the large boxes and the mattress packing to the garage, though he had clearly expressed his displeasure at having to take part in the work. As he passed the dining room window, I saw him stop and stare up at the roof, watching, I was sure, the parrots who lived in our olive trees.

He made several more trips. Then he appeared in the dining room doorway. "Should our roof be on fire?"

We raced out the door and looked up. Our wood-shingle roof was covered with ivy, dried now by the winter. The tendrils grew down inside the chimney, and the heat from the fireplace had ignited them. All the ivy was in flames.

We ran to get the ladder and Ron climbed onto the roof. We threw him the garden hoses from both the front and back yards, and he sprayed the fire frantically, working closer and closer to the chimney. Suddenly he screamed, *"Snakes!"* He had stepped into a nest of them—the living creatures that most terrified him—wintering on the roof. Jumping wildly to frighten them off, or just because he was terrified to put his feet down, he managed to douse the burning ivy. Covered with soot and carbon, soaking wet and shaking, he descended from the roof to join us.

Two men, strangers, stood in the center of our yard, watching us, their arms folded across their paunches. "Hiya, I live right next door," the bigger one said. "Boy, you're real lucky. You coulda had a real bad one there! I'm a fireman, and I oughta know."

So we had our California home.

———————

My relationship with Marcia did not improve. One night I was home alone when she phoned. "Hello, Sean, is your father there?"

"What do you want?"

"I'd like to speak with your father. Is he there?"

"No, he is not!" I said furiously. She wanted my dad, of course, not me.

"Do you know when he'll be back?"

"He'll never be back!" I shouted into the phone. I slammed it down. Suddenly I felt dizzy and lightheaded and the room began to shrink around me. I was filled with remorse and I felt sick. I had to call her back at once and apologize. Quickly I dialed the studio, but someone whose voice I didn't recognize answered. She wasn't there. Frantically I called her at home. I had to tell her I was sorry and that I loved her! The phone rang and rang. I listened to it for a long time before I gave up. I swore and screamed at it for not helping me, and then I burst into tears. I cried until I was completely exhausted. I knew that what I had been doing to her was wrong, that my behavior didn't make any sense. I couldn't do this any more.

My high school classes were easy, much easier than the ones I had taken in Ohio, and I didn't feel nearly as threatened as I had there. Still, I hated it when a teacher called on me in class, and I never volunteered answers because I didn't want to stand out. I was terrified of saying anything in front of a group of people, and I knew that if I was going to continue to make progress socially, I had to break the hold of my fear. So I signed up for a speech class.

The first time I had to walk to the front of the class and talk, I was nauseated, and my knees were shaking so badly I was sure I was going to fall down in front of everyone. When I tried to speak my voice was high and squeaky, and I hated the sound of it. They all sat and watched me. I knew that if the teacher hadn't been there, they would have burst out laughing and made fun of me. When I sat down I was humiliated and embarrassed. I knew I'd made a terrible mistake to take this class, but I refused to give in to my fear.

The second speech was no better. When it was over, the teacher told me that I had to stop clutching my arms when I spoke, that I had to relax. I looked at my arms and saw that they were covered with deep scratches.

By the end of the course it had become easier. I knew I had really accomplished something but realized I had expected much more—I had wanted to come out of that class able to be at ease in any social situation, and I had thought I'd have a sense of humor as well.

But I felt how I was changing. For the first time I was beginning to have control over my behavior. The person inside me was emerging, and I had the most bizarre feeling that I was somehow giving birth.

Now that it was really happening at last, I wanted everything to fall into place; I wanted to be whole. I was supposed to be funny, to be able to make sparkling conversation and dazzle people with my intelligence and humor. When something happened that showed me my picture wasn't true, I raged violently and threw things at my bedroom wall. There was no more time to waste!!

In the second semester I chose to take a class called "Coping." It was about problems teenagers had, and it turned out to be one of the wisest choices of my life. The teacher was a compassionate woman who was overtly affectionate with her students. She was as comfortable discussing birth control as my English teacher was with nouns and verbs. I felt at ease in her presence, and no one was judged, no matter what they said. She had a positive effect on the students, and they were extremely supportive with one another.

We discussed a wide range of topics, and one day the subject of autism came up. She described the symptoms and behavior of the disease; it was as if she were talking about me, as if somehow she knew what went on inside my head and was telling the class about it without using my name! Was she using me as a model? I said nothing, but I sat at my desk feeling as if I had been turned inside out for everyone to look at. What the hell was going on?!

I told nobody about my bizarre experience in class. But three days later I had another experience, and this one changed my life.

A friend phoned to tell me that there was a movie on television called "Son Rise," a true story about an autistic child and his family. "You should watch it," she said, "and maybe Sean should too."

Ron and I had told Sean that he was autistic when he was ten years old—we explained as simply as we could that it was something he couldn't help, that it caused him to do the things he did. He paid no attention whatever, then or any of the other times since, though we continued to explain that his behavior was in control of *him*. It was a confusing message, though, because that very behavior was what we were constantly asking *him* to *control*.

I turned on the television and called Megan and Sean, and together we watched the movie. The five-year old boy in the film had the same compulsions as Sean at that age—the spinning, the twirling, the self-hypnosis. During the first commercial Sean went to the kitchen for a drink. "It's amazing," Megan said. "He's exactly like Sean was!" Sean came back and sat down; he seemed restless, but he continued to watch the movie with us.

The mother's method of getting through to her child, I saw, was to enter his world with him as a way of eventually bringing him out. She joined him in spinning a plate, over and over; she flapped her hands just the way he did, for hours at a time. And little by little, almost imperceptibly, it worked; he began to notice her, to look at her, to respond. And after months of having his mother sit with him and copy him, the little boy emerged from his autistic behavior to become a normal child. It was a moving and triumphant story; my eyes filled with tears, and I had to choke back sobs. But why hadn't this happened to us? Every time we gave in to Sean's compulsions and didn't try to interrupt his repetitious behavior, he got worse. Had we done what this woman had, he would have slipped away completely.

———

I sat and watched this kid on television. I was fascinated. The more I saw, the closer the similarities were between him and me. He did the same things I had always done, and I couldn't believe my eyes! He was fascinated with spinning objects, with chains, all of it! For the first time in my life I saw another person like me! I said nothing as we watched the show—I wanted to wait until it was over to find out if what I suspected was true.

But by then I was too scared to ask my question, the thing I wanted most in the world to know. How would Mom react? What if she got mad and thought I was only asking something I already knew? My feelings were very mixed up—I felt a little sick, yet at the same time I had a growing sense of relief, a funny kind of peacefulness inside me. Could it be that what made me like this was a disease of some kind and that I was not a horrible person after all? I had to take the risk.

"Mom," I said, "I'm autistic too, aren't I?"

"Yes," she said. We sat very still and looked at each other for a long, long time. I had the strangest feeling, one that was entirely new to me. All at once I knew that I could ask Mom anything, say anything I wanted, and that it would be all right—she would understand me. Inside me a dam burst open. I knew I could use words like everybody else.

"Mom, why have you and Dad yelled at me all my life when I never meant to do anything wrong?"

"Because we didn't know what else to do. We tried everything to make you stop what you were doing. Sean, do you remember what you were like when you were very small?"

"Of course. I remember everything."

I stared at him. I couldn't take my eyes from his. I had never seen his face before, not like this. It was relaxed, thoughtful, unguarded. And we were talking to each other! My seventeen-year-old son and I were having the first real conversation of our lives. I was terrified to move.

"Then you remember doing those same things—the crayons, the chains, all that stuff, year after year. What were you doing?"

"It was all the same," he said. "Those were the things that gave me pleasure."

I waited. "That was it?"

He smiled. "That was it."

"But what did you think when Dad and I kept trying to stop you, when we screamed at you and punished you?"

"I thought you hated me."

My chest burned. "Did you understand that it was what you *did* that we hated, not you?"

"No."

"But they were dangerous, destructive things—we *had* to try and stop you!"

"I see that now."

"Do you know how much I hated yelling at you, spanking you, being angry with you?"

"Now I do, yes."

"Sean, do you know I love you?"

"Yes. I love you too."

Mom and I talked for hours. I'd never felt anything like it before. I really looked at her as we spoke, and I became aware of the enormous stored-up pain inside me. Part of the pain was for me, the other part for her.

"I never wanted to hurt you," I said, "but now I know that

I've been hurting you for years and years. I didn't know how to stop."

This conversation turned things around between Mom and me. When we were both finished talking, we held each other. Neither one of us wanted ever to let go. I wanted to hold on until all the pain inside me was released and I was free.

I went on a crusade. I took a look at myself in a way I had never done before, and this is what I saw: I had problems, real ones, big ones. But that didn't mean that there was something fundamentally wrong with me, that I was unlike everybody else in the world. I knew that I was separate from the problems I had and that I could overcome them. I declared war! I was going to fight against all the behaviors I had obeyed all my life. Since playing cards were a major temptation to me, I threw away all my decks of cards and told my mother what I was doing and why. Dead-end streets and bus numbers still went round and round in my head, and I pushed them out—I made myself think other thoughts instead.

I began to separate things. I made a list of the things I was terrified of and figured out how to conquer my fears. I had believed for so long that I was abnormal, retarded, inferior; now I realized I didn't feel that way anymore. It was very hard to make the changes I knew I had to make, and I got furious with myself whenever I saw that I had fallen short of my goals.

When I started coming alive, I had a deep desire to do something to help other people. My "Coping" teacher suggested that I volunteer as an aide at a neighborhood nursing home, and I did just that. I loved those patients. I read their mail to them, took them to various activities, and spent a lot of time talking and listening to them. They responded to me and really liked me. I was frightened at first of what

232

the patients would think of me, but after a few days I knew I had done the right thing, and it made me feel wonderful.

During my senior year in high school the relationship between Mom and me really blossomed. I began going to her and telling her things that were on my mind. She gave me praise and encouragement, and my feelings of self-worth grew. Now that we were getting along so well, I wanted the feelings between us to be perfect. I wanted her never, ever to correct me or to get impatient or angry—I demanded total control over my behavior and wanted to squelch all my impulses to do things I knew would make her angry. It wasn't so easy. Every time we did have an argument, I was deeply wounded and believed that the progress I had made was being reversed. Now, instead of getting furious with her, I got angry with myself. She explained that I could get angry with her, that she made as many mistakes as I did, that when I was mad at her I should tell her so. But at the time, I turned all my anger against myself.

I had so much to learn, so many things to change. I was shockingly conditioned, "trained," to respond negatively to Sean, to assume he was teasing me, trying to anger me, to use me as a set piece in his behavior patterns. A new person was emerging, vulnerable and hesitant. I had to stop reacting as I had for so long—the anger flashing out of me before I knew it was coming. I'd see the wounded look on Sean's face as he withdrew from me, another of his attempts to chart out safe territory ending with an explosion.

I'd grab him then, pull him back to me, apologizing for my insensitivity and telling him I had misunderstood. Sometimes, many times at first, the old behaviors came back and he was swept away again, his eyes expressionless, the familiar giggle when nothing was funny. But always, now, there was an end to it; we could get him back.

There was so much he didn't know, a world he had missed and that had to be explained to him slowly, painfully, carefully. We talked so long and so often that I frequently found myself with a sore throat, my voice hoarse. Ron and I described relationships among people, simple cause-and-effect behavior that he learned as if by rote, but remembered. He was beginning to learn in one situation and carry the learning over to another situation entirely.

It was June 1980 and I was graduating from high school. I was thrilled and proud because I knew what a huge accomplishment it was for me. After the ceremony my parents had a big party for me at home. I stood in the dining room and looked around at all the people. I realized they were all there because of me, and I was filled with jubilation. I could hardly believe this was me!

I decided to go to college. I had always thought it would be impossible for me, so I hadn't really given it any thought. Now my feeling was quite different—I believed I could do anything I wanted. I found a school I liked not far from our home and decided to study elementary education. When I got there I found the atmosphere relaxed and welcoming. I found my way around very quickly and was happy to see that the work was comprehensible and not too difficult. I lived at home and took a bus to school.

Once I got used to my classes and knew I could do all right, I decided to try and get a job so I could make some money of my own. Since I liked little kids, I decided to go for an interview at a preschool nearby. I was extremely nervous at the interview, but I struggled to appear confident and relaxed. I told myself not to be furiously disappointed if I didn't get the job. I could hardly believe it when the director said I was hired. I felt as if I would burst before I got home to tell Mom and Dad the news. They were both there when I arrived, and they were thrilled and proud of me; we went out to dinner to celebrate.

There was one big problem, however, with both college and my new job: transportation. The LA bus system was completely unreliable, and besides, everyone I knew except me had a driver's license. Megan had been driving for more than a year, and I wanted to get a license, too. I had discussed the subject several times with my parents, and they felt that I should wait a "little longer" before I learned to drive. Now Mom and I talked about it again. She said she was afraid I would lose my temper and have an accident (when I got angry I was still quite uncontrollable). She also said that because I still set up rules for myself that were often impossible for me to follow, I should probably wait a while before I tried to drive. I had to admit I knew what she meant and that I agreed with her; I, too, was a little afraid of what I might do when driving a car. But as time went on and I felt myself able to control my responses and reactions, I became determined to learn to drive.

I looked in the phone book and found a driving instructor. Without saying anything to Mom or Dad, I hired him and paid for the lessons myself. I found it easy to drive and caught on quickly. When Mom and Dad were in New York for a few days I took the driving test and passed it the first time. When they came home I told them what I'd done. They were both surprised and happy for me. Mom told me I was obviously capable of making up my own mind about what I could and couldn't do and that she had been wrong to discourage me. She and Dad told me they were thrilled with me not only because I'd learned to drive but also because I had made the decision myself and overcome a problem on my own.

In spite of my almost miraculous progress I still couldn't tolerate the inconsistency of my own mind. If I could do some things, why not everything? I had begun to triumph over very difficult obstacles, but it was often the simple ones that stopped me cold.

* * *

Sean came home one afternoon from his job as teaching assistant at the preschool. He was quite upset, angry with himself. He avoided me and went right to his room. I followed.

"Sean, what is it? You're having a problem at work?"

"No. I'm fine."

"But I can see that's not true. Tell me."

After a silence he burst out, "It's those goddamned bows—any idiot can tie a bow!"

But he couldn't. The kids had made masks for Halloween, and he and the teacher had fitted them with string and tied them on. The teacher had said repeatedly, "Tie bows, Sean, you're tying them in knots and they won't come off." He had tried, over and over, but he had no idea how to tie a bow that was not on his own shoe.

"So what? I'll teach you right now and then you will know how."

"I'm nineteen years old and can't tie a bow?!! That means I'm a moron!"

"It means you had other things going on while the rest of the kids learned to tie bows! Come on, stop feeling sorry for yourself and watch so you learn right now."

"But everybody in the world can do this except me!" He shook his head in exasperation.

"Look—you were so caught in your repetitive behavior that you didn't know what the hell was going on. You've had a life of severe problems that other kids didn't have, and you've pulled yourself out of them. You have to face the fact that you've missed an awful lot that everybody else learned when they were very young. So learn it now!"

He looked at me as if weighing what I'd said. "Sean, there's going to be a lot of this. The important thing is that you can't hide what you don't know, pretending you do. Just come to me, or to Dad, and ask. I mean if you'd been blind and suddenly at the age of seventeen had your sight restored, someone would have to teach you what everything is—the names of the colors, for instance. It's the same thing! There's nothing to feel embarrassed about. Okay?"

"Okay."

Ron and I had this conversation with Sean hundreds of times. His sense of confidence, of self-esteem, was so elusive and fragile. Perhaps the hardest thing for him was exposing what he really didn't know; after all, he was looking out for the first time at a world he had barely noticed before. In a way, everything was equal to him—he got as angry with himself for not knowing how a car engine worked as he did at his ignorance of the word for a baby cow. He had no way of distinguishing between what he "should" know at his age and what most people never do know. Everything had to be explained.

We were amazed that along with the rest of the personality that was emerging in our son was a distinct sense of humor. He'd given up trying to tell jokes—he even said he realized it wasn't a talent that ran in the family—and instead he was becoming truly funny, sarcastic at times, even self-mocking. Little by little we found that we could tease him and that he could tease back, his laugh a new sound to all of us.

The changes in Sean were miraculous, and we could see them happening every day. He watched everything and everyone, asking questions nonstop.

He seemed to have been unaware that he was a member of a family and that families functioned in similar ways—the fact that other parents corrected their kids, yelled at them, disciplined them was a revelation to him and a shock. "But how could I not have known this?" he asked, baffled.

As I grew to know my son I was taken aback by the kind of person he was. For seventeen years he had appeared to be destructive, negative, self-absorbed, insensitive—heartless. Now I saw a young man whose eyes filled with pain if a remark he made was misunderstood, if he did even the least thing to displease us. He reacted with sorrow and indignation to the mistreatment of children who attended the school where he was a teaching assistant. He began reading newspapers and was horrified by the personal and political crime that was everywhere. He grew more and more amazed at the way people behaved with one another. "But why can't they *change!?*" he'd say as I tried to explain inexplicable human behavior. (And why *not?*—after all, he had.)

His earlier fixation with criminals, he explained, had been the result of his conviction that someday the impulses that drove him would spin out of control and that he, too, would become a murderer and spend the rest of his life in prison.

He bought an old car and learned how to take care of it, doing many of the minor repairs himself. He began to collect vintage jazz records and in no time knew all the musicians and the groups they had played with. But this time he didn't "display" his knowledge the way he always had before, the way, I'd read, most autistic kids did as a substitute for real conversation. When he found someone who shared his interest in jazz, he talked enthusiastically about his favorite players; otherwise, his pleasure was in the music and reading about the lives of the people who played it. He bought himself a trumpet and hired a teacher so that he could learn to play well enough to appreciate the music he loved even more.

But the progress was never even. I got furious when I found he had used my soup kettle to change the oil on his car. "But *you* put oil in it when you cook, so why are you *angry!?*" he flashed back at me.

There was no sudden "awakening," no clap of thunder that changed our son into a "normal" person. It was hard work and it took time. Everything had to be named, its function described. Many things still do.

We were faced with another major change. After five years in Los Angeles, we were moving to New York. Our friend Maureen McGovern, the singer Ron managed and for whom I wrote songs, had been given the lead in a Broadway musical. She would be in New York for at least a year, probably much longer, and in order to continue working together, we would have to be there, too.

Megan, having completed her second year at UCLA as a French and Persian major, decided to come with us. Sean, however, said that he wanted to move back to Ohio, to our hometown. Ron and I were horrified.

"But you hated it there! Why would you go back?"

"I need to go back now, that's all."

I couldn't allow him to make such an obvious mistake! I tried to stop him, to talk him out of it, since I knew beyond doubt that it was the worst thing he could do. The old temptations would pull him back into his old behavior patterns. People there knew him the way he had been, and they wouldn't see the changes—he would become again what they still thought he was. I talked and I argued, pleading that he use common sense. "You'll go back there and ruin your life. There aren't even any jobs!" I cried. "All the steel mills are closed and everyone is out of work—it's the worst unemployment in the country!"

He listened to it all but insisted, "I have to prove to myself I can do it."

———

My parents and my sister were moving to Manhattan. I didn't want to live there because the size of the city was intimidating, and everyone seemed very different from me. I had no connection with New York. I decided, instead, that I wanted to return to Ohio, to the town where I had grown up. I had an overwhelming desire to "make up" for the years when Ohio was a word that caused me acute pain. I knew very well that I couldn't change what had happened, but I also knew I had the power to overcome the past with the present. I desperately needed to replace the memory I had of being a pathetic, lost kid, afraid of everything in his life, with the man I had become.

So in March 1984 I fulfilled what I thought of as a mission. I knew I was taking a tremendous risk that could mean catastrophe and reverse some or all of the progress I had made up to that point, but I was determined to do it.

Dad, Megan, and I drove our belongings across the country while Mom flew ahead to find me an apartment. I arrived in my home-town with a bundle of high hopes. I knew that returning here after six years of major progress in my own life would make me a hero. Grandpa was probably getting ready to assemble a cast of relatives for my homecoming. I couldn't wait! I was a totally different person, and I knew everyone would see all the changes in me and be overwhelmingly impressed. They would accept me at once.

Within a few days I had moved into my new apartment. I was now a resident on a quiet street two miles from my childhood home. At last I had real independence, with everyone at my fingertips; for the first time I was on my own (my God, on my own!)—no parents and no sister competing for attention from other people. I would *savor the spotlight myself! I was home, and I knew that in no time I'd find a group of friends, a job, and complete acceptance.*

Mom, Dad, and Megan left for New York, and soon afterward uncertainty began to creep in. Where was my hero's welcome? What about the homecoming? Shit, where was the goddamned welcome mat? I was alone in my apartment and no one called. It's still too soon, I told myself. Perhaps many people don't even know I'm here! But Grandpa will tell them and pretty soon everyone will know. Just give them time, Sean, I thought, and the phone will be ringing off the hook—every time I turn around it will be, "Hi, Sean, this is Aunt Mary. We're thrilled you're home; let's get together soon!" And "Sean! It's so good to have you home again. The kids are tickled, too, and can't wait to see you . . ." My celebrity status would soon be confirmed once everyone became aware of my valorous move.

Several days passed. A week went by. No one called me except Grandpa and then only to discuss some car insurance. There sat the phone, looking like the black box it was, while I sat in the deafening silence of my apartment feeling more and more like a black hole. The television and the radio were my only companions while time pressed forward, leaving me in the dust. A well of anger grew in me. Had I sacrificed all my friends, my security, and the progress I'd made for this life of invisibility? Maybe if I turned on my garbage disposal and stuck my hand in, someone would notice and perhaps—just perhaps—the phone would ring. But would anyone care?

After a month or so of looking for work, I managed to find a part-time job in a doughnut store—minimum-wage janitorial work. I could think of few euphemisms for "janitor," but that didn't stop me from trying: Extended doughnut shop service? Restorative shop care? So, I thought, this is what I went through twelve years of school and three years of college for! I worked alone for three hours every evening, so my schedule gave me no opportunity to meet anyone.

After a few hours of unrewarding work, I would return to my empty apartment. The phone became my enemy.

Two months passed and nothing changed. One day in April I was pulled out of my apartment when Maynard Ferguson, a great jazz trumpeter, came to town for a concert. I had to go and see him, so I went alone. It was a spectacular night and Ferguson was everything I'd hoped he would be. Members of the audience swayed back and forth, addicted to his music, as I was. There was, however, a tumorlike darkness growing inside me, and I became sharply aware of it during the concert. Maynard Ferguson was a major hero in Boardman; this was obvious by the crowd's enthusiastic response to his every move. But what about me? Wasn't I just as heroic for moving back to Ohio despite my painful past? Okay, so I couldn't hit a high C on the trumpet. I was a different kind of hero from Ferguson, but certainly no less courageous; after all, who else would have done what I'd done and faced up to a background of pain and problems? As I scanned the audience and watched their response, I realized I was the only person who had come alone. I didn't even know anyone I could have asked, and the days of walking through the school halls with my head down came rushing back to me with painful clarity. Was I doomed to succumb to the past?

I loved the concert, but I emerged heavy with dismay and hopelessness and angry as hell. I went home feeling that this was going to be my life from now on, living alone, unnoticed. I had no friends and knew of no place to meet any.

Loneliness had its hands around my neck and was squeezing hard. The only thing that helped was calling my mother on the phone, which I did frequently. She was my lifeline, even though my conversations with her were peppered with the ugly injustices of my life: no friends, no job, no girlfriend. Mom was on hand to cheer me up or at least to lessen the cancerous darkness inside me. She did every-

thing she could to assuage my loneliness and help me see beyond myself. I could share anything I wanted to with her, anything, that is, except one important topic—under no circumstances could I admit that moving back to Ohio had been a bad decision. It was impossible for me to say I'd made a fatal mistake and confirm that my mother had been right. The decision, though, was one I'd absolutely had to make; the alternative was a lifetime of uncertainty and unfulfilled needs—I had to do what I set out to do; otherwise I would never be a success.

When fall finally came I entered Youngstown State University to continue my education. I had decided to major in early-childhood education because I had worked with small children in Los Angeles and felt that a degree in the field would lead to a brighter, more secure future. I signed up for the required courses, but frustration was already there, waiting to claim me.

I felt totally out of place as soon as I walked into the first class and sat down. In fact, I was to find that all my classes had one common element—I was the only male in any of them! Christ, what was going on here? I'd seen no "Women Only" signs posted on the doors, but I felt as if I'd invaded a women's club. After the initial shock, however, I thought that perhaps being in classes with all women would make it easier to find someone I could ask out—I certainly didn't have any competition! When I walked into my classes, however, I felt so conspicuous that I pretended not to notice I was the only guy in sight.

Another problem at school was that it was mainly a commuter college. Students went to class and then directly home, so there were few opportunities to meet anyone. I could see that I was in for a great year!

I went through the days angry and sometimes livid; I was met with failure at every turn. But slowly, the rage became transformed into determination, and I vowed to myself: "I am going to make it no matter what!" I decided to branch out and investigate which student groups pertained to my interests. I found one right away; it was called "Students United for Peace," and it met twice a week.

At the first meeting there were three people present. Two of them, I could tell at once, had difficulty relating to other people. Further complicating matters was the fact that the whole campus was apathetic about the arms race—there were no nuclear warheads swirling in the sky over Youngstown State's campus, so why spend time worrying about what probably would never happen anyway?

I pressed onward, but not upward. I remained fairly active with the peace group, though I was fighting for a cause no one cared much about and making no friends in the process. Next I looked into the university's extracurricular activities.

Why hadn't I thought of this before? Both bowling and volleyball were offered—the two sports I loved the most because they were the only ones I was not terrible in. I'd struck gold—what a great way to have fun and meet people! When I inquired, however, I was astonished to learn that bowling had been cancelled for the quarter and volleyball was on hiatus due to a lack of interest.

My feelings of hopelessness, anger, and despair were so intense at times that all I wanted was to move back to California and resume the life I had led there. I could annul my dead-end life in Ohio and go on with what I'd had before. The only calls I made were long-distance, either to my parents in New York or to my friends in Los Angeles; even my grandfather rarely called me, so why would anyone miss me if I left again?

Then suddenly, I got a taste of the intimacy I craved so much—one of my friends from LA came and stayed with me for a week. I felt pampered and a little spoiled, and it was wonderful! The two of *us even made a one-day trip to New York to visit my family. When she returned to California and I to my empty apartment, I had fallen in love with her.*

After she left I was even lonelier. I had only my grandfather as a friend and companion, and when I went to visit him we talked about sports, TV shows, and his friends. I clearly saw that this was all I had in my life, and I found myself resenting him for it because I knew he wasn't really interested in me. Also, he had money and I had virtually none, since my job at the doughnut store paid almost nothing. One night when I was visiting him, a volatile mix of anger and desperation flooded through me. I opened his medicine cabinet, took out a bar of soap and a stick of deodorant, and dropped them into my pocket. He has so many of each, I reasoned, that he won't notice or care if one or two items are gone. How wrong I was!

It was a few days before I stopped in again to visit him. After an hour or so he invited me to stay for dinner. We sat at the kitchen table and he talked about a television show he'd watched, while I half listened. Then a heavy silence filled the air and he spoke very matter-of-factly. "Sean, I want to tell you something that I don't like to mention, but you brought it on yourself." Trembling inside, I squeaked out, "What is it?"

"Did you take some things from my bathroom?"

"Yes," I gasped. I felt short of breath. "I won't sit here and lie to you. I did take them, but I didn't think you'd notice."

Impatiently, he said, "Of course I noticed! I just used the deodorant that morning—I would notice something like that missing!"

I was so filled with guilt I felt sick. I explained that I'd been feeling desperate; that my financial situation was terrible and I'd received two notices from the bank that week because I'd overdrawn my checking account. I added that I knew I had no excuse for stealing from him—from my own grandfather of all people!

He said, "I understand, Sean, but you shouldn't have taken those things, see, because I won't know if I can ever trust you again." I sat there in a sea of shame, his words burning my insides. How could I have stooped so low?

A few days later I was fired from my job at the doughnut shop when the owner hired a relative of his in my place. I was alienated from everyone, trapped in a lake under a frozen surface. I knew that I couldn't go on this way, that I was drowning in self-pity. I was furious with myself for the state I was in. I had to change it, now, before it was too late; I had to get beyond my own narrowing world.

I decided to volunteer at a crisis intervention center connected to the university. I was told that each volunteer had to complete a five-week training course and receive certification before being allowed to work the phones. Fine, I thought; I can handle that.

The class was very informal and relaxed but well structured. Volunteers had to be nonjudgmental, compassionate, and empathetic—all attributes I felt I possessed. At last, I thought, I would be able to use my sensitivity to benefit others and in so doing benefit myself.

I "graduated" from the course after five weeks. We were taught how to handle a wide range of problems—from what agency to recommend to someone who was hungry to how to deal with a potential suicide. A few weeks later I was certified to work the phones alone.

Besides becoming certified, I'd also made progress in another way; I'd met my first friend in the volunteer class. Greg was a guy with a carefree attitude toward life, just the type of person I needed to get me out of myself. He was gay, and although I knew very little about the gay life-style, his sexual orientation was never an issue *with respect to our friendship. Shortly after I met him he introduced me to Karen, who also became a friend. She pronounced herself a peace activist, and the buttons and emblems she covered herself with confirmed where she stood. Karen said that she wanted a harmonious world, and her resentment toward the establishment was often fierce. At once I knew I would like this woman for sure—no doubt about it!*

"She has a temper and can fly off the handle for no reason," I was warned. "She has a very unstable home life," someone else said. I blotted out the warnings; after all, I needed friends, friends, friends, and I didn't give a damn about her temper. I reasoned that everyone had faults and that once she'd been exposed to me and the person I had become, she would probably soften.

Soon I was spending most of my time with Karen. She grew more and more dependent on me at a time when I desperately needed to be needed. If she wanted something from me, as long as I could provide it, it was hers. Our friendship was a learning experience I was not likely to forget.

As time passed I began to admit to myself that my friendship with Karen was becoming strained. If she needed to go somewhere, I had to drive her. If she needed to talk—even if it was about the same old problems I'd listened to countless times before—I was all ears. I began to realize I was being used, and I didn't like the feeling. Her outbursts of temper were frequent and violent; it became clear to me that I was not going to "save" Karen, that I would only be dragged down into her problems. I began to realize that this was not the kind of friendship I needed; I'd begun to put a little trust in myself. I stopped being there when Karen called, and I said I was busy if she needed me to drive her somewhere. Eventually, I crawled out from under the friendship into the fresh air.

Working at the crisis center, meanwhile, was pulling me out of

249

myself. I spent my weekly four hours on the phone hearing from people with all kinds of problems: alcohol, drugs, child abuse, relationships marked with violence and fear. Sometimes the caller spent half our conversation crying. A few just needed to unload their troubles. Many had overwhelming family pressures and no money. I had spent nearly all my life unable to imagine what I could not directly see, and now, for the first time, I was getting a taste of what real problems were. I was profoundly shocked. There had been times in my own life when I'd wanted to commit suicide, but fear of the unknown had always stopped me. Now I was talking to people in trouble, and not all of them saw suicide as the only way out. This realization opened my eyes, and my perspective about my own life began to change. How could I have thought my problems were so huge?

My life at the university inched forward while I let things just happen to me. I was becoming increasingly burdened by something I refused to admit even to myself: I no longer had any enthusiasm about becoming a daycare teacher. I was trapped in my predicament because I had no idea what I wanted to do instead. I felt obligated to follow the path of least resistance, doing nothing about it, and I was ashamed of myself; after all, my parents were shelling out the money every quarter to fund my education. Since I couldn't earn enough to put myself through school, how could I switch my major when that would mean more classes, more time, more money? So I said nothing.

Toward the end of 1985 I met Lynne, a young woman I really liked and was very attracted to. Soon I found myself sitting by the phone trying to work up the courage to call her. The first two times I hung up before the call went through, but on the third try I reached *her. She remembered me clearly and, like a sick person trying to swallow a foul-tasting pill as quickly as possible, I asked her out. She said yes and proceeded to give me directions to her house. I felt awash with relief, and somewhere deep down I knew that if I was to have a girlfriend soon, she would be the one.*

I was elated until the time came for me to pick her up. Suddenly nervousness consumed me. Didn't most women judge a prospective date very closely? What if she decided within thirty seconds that I just didn't fit the bill? I felt as if I was walking on eggshells and that one slip would shatter everything—even unkempt hair would be grounds for dismissing me from her life. How did I know if I looked right? What would I say to her?

I began to tell myself that I was generally a good person. Why wouldn't she want to date me? After all, nasty, foul-mouthed, potbellied men could be seen in public all the time with dates, girl-friends, and wives! I will be a winner, I thought, by just being myself with her. I hoped.

Our first date was a success, and Lynne and I began to go out often. From the outset I was determined that ours would be a relationship of equality; I vowed always to treat her as well as I possibly could. From time to time small difficulties arose, as in any relationship, but they were mainly a result of my not having learned certain social behaviors.

At Christmas my family came to town for the holidays; I took Lynne to my grandfather's house to spend the evening with everyone and get to know them. When we'd been there awhile I left the living room and went downstairs to the basement to play pool, alone. I didn't give a thought to leaving Lynne upstairs to visit with my parents and Megan. After all, she was a permanent fixture in my life, and I saw nothing wrong with going off by myself for awhile. I found, however, that I had miscalculated.

"Sean, where have you been?" Mom asked with surprise two hours later when I came back upstairs.

"What? I . . . I was down playing pool. I hadn't played for a long time and I . . ."

"But what about Lynne? You can't just leave her upstairs by herself. She hardly knows us and she feels very awkward—I think she's very upset that you abandoned her."

"But why? She seemed to be having a good time, so I didn't see any harm in leaving her up here."

Mom had calmed down and was making it much easier for me to settle my feelings and get off the defensive. "Sean, she feels out of place because she's never been here before. You have to be with her and be responsible for her since you're the one she has the relationship with," she said soothingly.

At that moment I had a tremendous revelation. For the first time I realized that I—Sean Barron—was responsible for another person. It was up to me to look after her welfare as much as I could. Until now I had barely been able to accept responsibility for myself and my own actions; now I had two people to think about, and I knew I had made a mistake. "I'm really sorry, Mom," I said. "I didn't mean to hurt her—I had no idea I was doing anything wrong."

Noticeably absent from this conversation were elements that had dominated the way Mom and I had talked to each other all my life. I didn't blow what she said out of proportion, nor did I use every weapon in my arsenal to defend my actions. This time I simply admitted my poor judgment, and I was a little humbled in the process. Mom explained that there was nothing wrong with me for being ignorant of certain social graces, that these were things I didn't know simply because I hadn't learned them. "People learn all their lives, Sean, if they're interested and really alive; there's no time limit."

With painstaking effort I graduated from the university in June 1987. Even though I no longer had any intention of working in the field, I received my degree in early-childhood education. Megan graduated from New York University at the same time, so Mom and Dad threw a party for both of us at my grandfather's home in Ohio. The party made me feel wonderful. I only wished that I were able to redo my college years and make them resentment-free. There were a lot of things I would have done differently, time I would not have wasted feeling sorry for myself.

After years of worrying about it, I finally told my parents how I felt about not wanting to work in child care. I was amazed to find that they were not in the least upset by the information. "That's not surprising," Dad said. "We don't know many people who actually work in the field they studied in school. Find out what you're interested in—you can always go back to the university for a master's degree or take other courses when you decide what you want."

By this time Lynne and I had become even closer, and our relationship had progressed to the point where I felt that I could take the risk and tell her about my autism. It was hard for me to do; after all, it was not a subject I had ever discussed with anyone except my parents. However, when I'd explained to her what my childhood had been like and described the person I had been, it made no difference to her. She loved me, she said, because of the person I was and for the way I treated her.

After this I felt completely free to express myself with Lynne. There was a wide disparity between us in terms of our experiences and backgrounds, but I saw this as enriching to our relationship. She had been born and lived her whole life in a tiny provincial town in Ohio and had never traveled. I, on the other hand, had moved to California and back again and had visited many other places as well.

I realized at about this time that I was a feminist, and my desire for a completely equal relationship was in conflict with her strict Catholic background, which, as she saw it, reinforced women's subservience to men. I worked hard at encouraging her to express her own needs and feelings, something not really done in her family, and I tried to convince her that she could do whatever she wanted in life instead of letting a lack of confidence hold her back. She had grown up in a rigid environment, one in which you wore a smile and conformed to what others expected of you. My upbringing was the antithesis of hers: My parents had used every method available to encourage me to be honest about my feelings, whatever they were. For many years I had been terrified to do so, but now since I'd started to speak about my real feelings, I knew my life had changed drastically for the better.

Lynne and I were together for three years. Since we broke up I have begun dating again. I still find it terrifying to ask a woman out because I'm afraid she'll refuse, but I know now that I'm certainly not alone in that.

I work full-time in the rehabilitation department of a nursing home, a job that I love, and one day a week I volunteer at the Easter Seal Society, where I help Alzheimer's patients. Instead of teaching very young children, I have gone to the other end of the spectrum to work with the elderly.

I love my life here in Ohio. I live in a town I know well, a place where I'm comfortable, and every day there's a reminder of how much I've changed from that tortured little boy I was. I know quite well that my autism will always be part of me, that it isn't something I can expect to be "cured." I will always have to fight against old behaviors that taunt me, and I still struggle to convince myself that I am, like everyone else, allowed to make mistakes—and that when I do there is no neon sign blinking over my head with the words: Moron! Weird! Retard!

A year after I moved back to Youngstown, Mom and I were having lunch at a health-food restaurant when suddenly I heard a too-familiar sound. Excitedly I peered out the window as several school buses passed by. "What numbers are they?" Mom asked, smiling at me.

I felt hot with terror and nausea. I was reverting to my old, uncontrollable behavior! I said defensively, "It's not like that—I'm not thrilled by those buses the way I used to be! I'm not interested in them!"

She nodded and seemed to agree with me.

"I'm slipping backwards, aren't I? I'm letting my past grab on and hold me!"

"No, Sean, that's impossible. You're a different person now than you were then. You've proven you can control those impulses you used to have." She reached out and took my hand. "You couldn't behave that way anymore even if you wanted to. Once a chicken is out of the egg, you know, he can't go back in!"

I think the most difficult aspect of my autism in recent years was having to admit to myself how much I had to learn. I actually experienced two sets of formative years—the first as a small child and the second in the years following my "breakthrough." I had so much pent-up anger inside that once it started coming out, it was hard to handle. Why couldn't I just be normal since I'd already come this far? I wanted everything to just fall into place. Why did everything have to be such a struggle? I often became incensed at what I saw as an "upside-down pyramid"; I had the ability to accomplish something nearly impossible, like overcoming autism, but I failed at the simplest things—not knowing correct table manners, not knowing how to put on clothes that looked right together. But little by little I began to accept the person I am. Like a recovering alcoholic who can't have alcohol in the house, I don't own a deck of cards because I still find the temptation to "play buses" too great. I am on guard against old habits that lure me into old behaviors. The road to acceptance has been bumpy and arduous, but I have come to realize my own limitations. I see myself today as an optimist, a productive member of the world rather than a victim of it. I feel I am a fulfilled and whole person, not a collection of uncontrollable impulses, and I am happier than I have ever been in my life.

Last December I said to Mom, "Could I have some books for Christmas?" Before that I had always thought: Why bother trying to read when everyone else in my family has read thousands of books and I'll never catch up even if I read twenty-four hours a day for the rest of my life! Suddenly I'd realized I didn't have to catch up, that I didn't have to compare my accomplishments to theirs. I saw that I was only denying myself education and pleasure. Since then I read all the time and love discussing books with my mother. Recently she gave me a copy of Tobias Wolff's memoir, This Boy's Life, and it was a revelation—the author had grown up isolated and misunderstood, filled with the same raging anger and attraction for violence that I'd felt. I was autistic and he wasn't, but his feelings were so very much like mine.

When I think of my confused, tumultuous childhood, I wonder how we ever got through it. I look at the four of us today, a closer family than any other I know. Obviously, this would not have been possible if Mom and Dad had accepted the diagnosis of doom that was given to them years ago. Instead, my parents gave me the greatest gift I could ever receive—they stuck by me and never gave up on me. Also, I never gave up on myself.

My sister, Megan, and I are great friends, and I open my life to her because I know she understands and loves me. We spend a lot of time laughing, and we have wonderful times together. I still feel awful about the way I treated her when we were kids, but my actions from the past certainly don't affect our relationship now.

My father is a man I try very hard to be like; I admire the way he deals with other people—he is patient and kind in a job where most people behave very differently. He seems to know how to handle himself in any situation, and to me it appears he can do anything he wants to.

My relationship with my mother is spectacular. In a way it is like looking into a kaleidoscope—no matter which part I see, it works; each part makes the others even better. We talk to each other several times a week, and I know that I can tell her whatever I'm feeling without worrying about what she'll think of me. No matter how serious my problem or how awful I feel about the dangerous state of the world, I never fail to feel better after I've talked to her. She has an uncanny ability to help me gain a perspective on things.

Sometimes I sit and reflect on my life so far. I remember the fear that was always with me, the confusion, the chaos, and storminess of my life with my family. Images flicker through my head like lightning—Mom screaming at me, Megan in the kitchen before me and my blinding rage at her, the eight days when Dad stopped speaking to me, the looks on the faces of the other kids I went to school with. I think of all we went through together, my family and I, and I think we lived some sort of miracle.

AFTERWORD

The four-year process of writing this book has changed Sean in ways I would not have thought possible. His writing when we began was wordy, peppered with psychological phrases and jargon. As he began to read other people's work, he became dissatisfied with his own. He decided to rewrite everything. "I use too many words—it needs to be simpler, more direct, to really capture what I felt, who I was," he told me. "Most of the stuff I've written just gets in the way." I said maybe he was right.

"You know the real reason I was writing that way? It helped me keep a distance between me and my feelings—it was as if I was writing about someone else, and it wasn't as painful that way. I've got to change that—it *has* to be painful or it won't mean anything." So he dealt with the pain.

I wrote in New York, he in Ohio, and we got together frequently to collaborate. We talked endlessly on the phone. As I read what he'd written, I discovered much of the real story for the first time. I was overwhelmed by the logic of his mystifying behavior; so much of it had simply been a desperate attempt to communicate.

A few days ago he said, "The thing that amazes me most about having written this book is that my anger is gone. I've forgiven myself. I thought I'd never be able to do that."

I've read a lot of books on autism, from 1964 to the present. Even now the cause is unknown, though there is general agreement that its origin is biological, not psychological. One author, writing in 1989, said: "It is actually impossible for a child to become autistic because it was not loved sufficiently by its mother or because it feels threatened in its very life and identity."[6]

In 1972, when Sean was eleven years old, Dr. Leo Kanner, the man who coined the term *refrigerator parents,* appeared before the parent members of the National Society for Autistic Children and declared them innocent.[7] No one told me. And after eleven years, it was a little late anyhow. It was late for so many desperate mothers and fathers who had been blamed for their children's tragic disabilities. But many things are different now.

There is still no cure. Behavior management—reinforcing "good" behavior with rewards, punishing "bad" behavior with temporary deprivation—is used most often (along with a combination of other methods), and many autistic kids respond favorably to it. I asked Sean to read a description of the method. "If we had done that with you, do you think it would have worked?"

He shook his head. "I really don't see how. I never gave a damn about rewards and punishments. There was nothing I *wanted* after all—certainly not a food reward—and what could you have taken away from me?"

Who knows? I keep thinking I should have done things differently, but I'm still not sure what I could have changed. I should *not* have yelled, spanked, been enraged. "But you couldn't have allowed me just to do what I wanted," Sean said recently. "If you had, I know for sure I would have stayed inside myself forever. With all the fighting and screaming going on, I knew someplace in my head that you were trying to get me out—and anyhow, it was the only time I listened!"

Autism does not go away. As Uta Frith, an expert in the field, says, "It is not a disorder of childhood; instead it is a disorder of development. In adulthood, mental development is not only distorted and delayed but, if its aim is maturity, then this aim is never reached . . . existence remains curiously restricted and abnormal."[8]

The authors of *Autism: A Practical Guide for Those Who Help Others* explain that "all people with autism, even those with above-normal intelligence living relatively independently, [share] a difficulty with social relationships and the use of language."[9]

Yes, experts in the field set limits; they define a range of accomplishment and growth within which autistic people remain. I often think of the phrase "self-fulfilling prophecy," which we were warned about as teachers: "If you expect a student to be slow because of IQ-test results and past performance, then the student will never leave the slow track—the child will fulfill your expectations."

No one knows the limits of the human heart and spirit. Last night Sean called. "I can't stop reading that novel you gave me, *Affliction,*" he said. "The author has made the main character unbelievably compelling and real! He's a man who wants to love but just doesn't know how—every time he tries to show how he feels he makes a mess of it, and everyone misunderstands him; he just doesn't know what signals to use!"

We talked about a lot of things. Just before we hung up he said, "I'm afraid the friendship between Terry and me is over. (Terry is one of his oldest friends from LA.) We've grown apart in the last year or so, and we don't see things the same way anymore."

"What things?"

"Well, he's in business for himself now, and he seems to be getting more and more ruthless. He does things to make money that he would never have approved of a few years ago. And he has started making racist remarks—he never used to be like that! I'm just not comfortable with him anymore."

This is a new Sean. How does he know these things? Only a few years ago we were still explaining basic relationships to him; now he has begun giving us advice on our problems—good advice. The only thing I'm sure of is that our son is the strongest person I've ever known. His successful struggle against autism shows an unwavering courage at which I can only marvel.

AFTERWORD
Second Printing, 2002

When this book was first published, Sean and I went on tour to promote it, a different city each day, with seven or eight hours of interviews in each city, one after the other.

On the fifth day we were in Minneapolis. It was late and we had one more radio show before the drive to the airport. The host, a young woman with more-than-usual knowledge of autism, turned to me at one point and said, "Judy, will you describe behavior modification for those unfamiliar with the term?"

I opened my mouth to respond and suddenly my brain went to sleep. I couldn't summon even one tiny word in the English language. Panicked, I looked at Sean.

"I'd like to explain that, if I may," he said, smiling. And he did, briefly, clearly. As we left the station, Sean put his arms around my shoulders and grinned. "Don't thank me for saving your ass. It was the least I could do."

I started to laugh but found myself choking back sobs. Where had this young man come from? How could he possible be the autistic son I had known for twenty-eight years?

There were to be many experiences like that. There were national television talk shows—here in the U.S. and in France, England and Germany—when I would sit next to

Sean and watch him speak so articulately, with such humor and charm, that I would be overcome with emotion, barely able to pull myself together enough to speak around the lump in my throat. It didn't help that I often saw tears in the eyes of the shows' hosts as well.

Reading his own life in print changed Sean perhaps more than anything else. It gave him some distance from the pain of his earlier years and allowed a new perspective to develop. Being an author also connected him to a larger world. For the first time in his life, he has become part of the autistic community where he is sought after, asked advice, and booked for speeches all over the country.

So much about autism is still unknown and more money is desperately needed for research. When our book came out I was naïve enough to think that we'd be deluged with requests from doctors and other professionals wanting to study Sean, since recovery is so rare.

What we heard, however, was denial: "If he recovered, then he never was autistic."

One autism professional, whom I'll call Gary, arranged for Sean and me to speak at a fund raiser. At the cocktail party preceding the event, he said to me, "So who wrote the book, really?"

I looked at Sean, standing beside me, his face reddening in anger.

"We did. Sean and I."

Gary gave me a long look, a half smile on his face. "Oh, sure," he said over his shoulder as he turned and walked away.

So I've learned that the field of autism is territorial like any other. Some professionals are open, responsive, willing to try new things, and to function as a team with the parents; others have a vested interest in their own system and demand rigid adherence to their methods.

I am encouraged, however, by the thousands of people Sean and I have met, in person and through letters and phone calls—mostly parents of children with autism, parents who fight for the best care and education for their kids, and who are not intimidated by either the medical establishment or their school systems. They seem so much more confident than I was.

In the meantime, the mantle over the fireplace in Sean's living room is becoming crowded with awards. Among them are Volunteer of the Year and Man of the Year from the Big Brothers and Big Sisters in his hometown. He spends an afternoon a week working at an animal shelter. He regularly visits a local prison with a church group, which offers childcare to the families visiting inmates.

Our isolated and desperately unhappy boy has become a man, intimately aware of and connected to the world. It has been a long journey.

But what a journey it has been.

Judy Barron
Pennsylvania
December 2001

They who give it large names are liars, or
They are fools. More softly, you and I,
Slow to assert what we can never prove,
Wonder what algebraist, what dictator
Can teach us much of truth or tyranny.
Look at me. Do not speak. But this is love.

—"Dogma," BABETTE DEUTSCH[10]

REFERENCES

1. Bruno Bettelheim, *The Empty Fortress: Infantile Autism and the Birth of the Self* (New York: Free Press, 1972), 22.
2. Ibid., 23.
3. Ibid., 25.
4. Clara Claiborn Park, *The Siege: The First Eight Years of an Autistic Child* (Boston: Little, Brown & Company, 1967), 135.
5. Ibid., 141.
6. Uta Frith, *Autism, Explaining the Enigma* (Oxford: Basil Blackwell, 1989), 60.
7. Nancy J. Minshew, M.D., and James B. Payton, M.D., "New Perspectives in Autism, Part I," *Current Problems in Pediatrics*, Vol. 18 (October, 1988), 569.
8. Frith, 6.
9. John Gerdtz and Joel Bregman, *Autism: A Practical Guide for Those Who Help Others*, (New York: Continuum Publishing Company, 1990), 20–21.
10. Babette Deutsch, "Dogma," *Coming of Age* (Bloomington: Indiana University Press, 1959).

ABOUT THE AUTHORS

Judy Barron is a lyricist and a writer who divides her time between writing children's songs and books and painting floor cloths and faux finishes. She lives in Poland, Ohio.

Sean Barron is a graduate of Youngstown State University and has been a correspondent and copy editor for the *Youngstown Vindicator* for eighteen years.

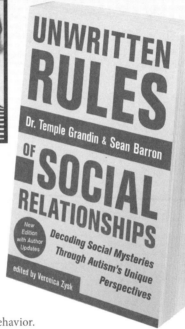